# Eating My
# *Secrets*

## Health/Healing/ Hope

## DEBRA MAZDA

Trilogy Christian Publishers A Wholly Owned Subsidiary of Trinity Broadcasting Network 2442 Michelle Drive Tustin, CA 92780

For information about special discounts for bulk purchases, please contact Trilogy Christian Publishing.

Manufactured in the United States of America

10 9 8 7 6 5 4 3 2 1

Library of Congress Cataloging-in-Publication Data is available.

ISBN 978-1-64088-245-4 (Paperback)
ISBN 978-1-64088-246-1 (ebook)

# Dedication

To my grandparents, Joe and Viola. Without them, who knows what would have happened to me. They were my greatest fans and loved me no matter what.

# Contents

# Acknowledgments

*T*here are so many people I need to thank, who have supported, inspired, and helped me to be a better person.

To all the women over the years, who so bravely and courageously poured out their hearts and souls and told me their stories.

To my very first therapist, who treated me as a patient with dignity over thirty years ago and told me that *it wasn't my fault*. That one, profound statement changed the course of my life. I will be forever grateful.

To my friend Elsa, whose friendship in those fragile years was invaluable to me. She gave me shelter, food, and a futon to sleep on during my brokenness, depression, and breakdown. She was wise enough to know I needed help. Both she and her dog never left my side. They were true angels from Heaven.

To Bernadette, who has shown me so much love over the years as we sat over many Caesar salads to discuss life and work.

To Angela, who has been a friend to me for over forty years and whose love, friendship, and support helped me get through the death of my beloved yellow lab, Hannah, in 2011, when I was not sure I would make it.

To Gere, whose support, honesty, and encouragement have given me another depth to my life and this book. When she died in 2012, a part of me went with her.

To Marie and Loretta, who were my partners in crime for years in Philly. They helped to keep my body in shape and are great friends to me.

To all my friends and family, who are special to me, love me with open hearts, and just let me be me.

But mostly, I want to say thanks to all my former *ShapelyGirl* Fitness members at my studio, who let me lead, teach, inspire, and motivate them. While they thought I inspired and motivated them, they pushed me to do better.

Last of all, I thank my Jesus, whose grace delivered and loved me enough to give me the strength and courage to fight for my life. He showed me that I could be whole again. It took me many years to see how I could turn this tragedy into a celebration, but He revealed it. I can now embrace the plan God has for me not only to give comfort, support, inspiration, and help to other women, but to let them know there is hope. Their future will not be determined by their past! If I had not experienced the pain, challenges, and struggles I have gone through, how was I to understand my Lord's!

*I waited patiently for the Lord;*
*And He inclined to me,*
*And heard my cry.*
*He also brought me up out of a horrible pit,*
*Out of the miry clay,*
*And set my feet upon a rock,*
*And established my steps.*
*He has put a new song in my mouth—*
*Praise to our God;*
*Many will see it and fear,*
*And will trust in the Lord.*
*Blessed is that man who makes the Lord his*
*trust,*
*And does not respect the proud, nor such as*
*turn aside to lies.*

*Psalms 40:1-4*

# Introduction

I am pretty sure I came out of the womb on some diet, because as far back as I can remember, diets were part of my life. In my teen years, as my weight began to increase, I was on a mission to lose it. I began reading about different diets, watched people get skinny on TV, or had girlfriends tell me about how many pounds they had lost with the newest diet. All these diets promised success, a thin body, and a better life. None of these diets worked, and I always gained the weight back once the diet ended.

By the time I was an adult, I pretty much crowned myself the Diet Queen. I took uppers and downers, drank weight-loss shakes, had cow's urine injected into my body, and even had my jaws wired shut — all to get rid of the fat that constantly reminded me of how imperfect I was. I felt bad about myself all day long. I was told by many that I had a pretty face; if only I could lose the weight. Being thin was on my mind day and night, and the battle was getting even harder.

My thoughts consisted of two things: *eating* all the time and how to *lose weight* for the last time. I had to get thin at any cost. Food was the comfort, friend, and relationship that I had; and until I got thin, that was not about to change. My weight was a constant struggle and battle. Losing weight was the goal, but dieting was so damaging physically, emotionally, and mentally.

Once I realized that dieting was getting me nowhere fast, I took matters into my own hands. I began to breathe and learned how to live. I started not only to eat better but befriended food. I realized I was in control. I had the power not the diet. No longer was I focused on negative thoughts about myself. While that was many years ago, and those days are far gone, today I live a very different life. Learning how to use food as fuel and nourishment for my body to move changed my life.

Constantly being bombarded with diets every day reminds you that you are less than perfect. Until you become thin, your life means nothing. The message is loud and clear, no matter which way you turn. It is time to stop *dieting* and start to own your life and live happier. In this book, I want to open a circle of friends to you. I pray that my story, with all its challenges and triumphs, will help you to reach deep down inside and start the process of healing your soul.

Telling the truth of my life, including my history of abuse and relationship to food, is the first step in mending the damage that has been inflicted on me and perhaps you. In addition, I offer a deeper understanding of the relationship between trauma, binge eating, and obesity. You do not have to be paralyzed by your past!

There are many paths to healing physically, emotionally, and spiritually. I found my own way a long time ago and work daily to stay on course. Now, I hope to blaze a trail for all who need to know they are not alone. They can be released from their secrets and shame and feel comfortable with their body. Never again will their weight prevent them from fulfilling their potential and finding peace.

# 1

## Eating My Secrets

Getting ready to start the Broad Street Run, a ten-mile race held in Philadelphia every May, I am getting myself psyched and motivated by listening to my iPod. I remind myself that I am not alone. I am part of my training team, who are with me and the other thirty thousand or so participants. I just want to finish this race, which is a personal challenge of mine. I am beginning to get very excited, scared, nervous, and tearful. While my heart is racing and my blood is pumping, I can feel my legs becoming like jelly. I just need to keep my eyes fixed on the journey before me.

I look ahead, not concerning myself with who is to my left, my right, in front, or back of me. I've done mindful training for a few years, and now it will surely pay off. That is my only reality. I need to run my race! With that in mind, I keep my eyes and thoughts focused ahead. I have programmed my mind to block out all negativity and replace it with an upbeat philosophy to put one foot in front of the other. For the next ninety or so minutes, I must block out everything that has ever held me back or tried to derail the dreams I desire to achieve.

As the leader of Team *ShapelyGirl* Fitness, this is not an individual event for me. For the past two months, I've been training a group of ten unlikely female runners of every shape and size. There are only three women on the team besides me who are less than two hundred pounds. While they are all up for the challenge physically, I need to make sure that motivation is what drives them to push further. They are depending on me to show them how to put their visual and mental training skills to work. I tell them to find their inner athlete and just shine. My mantra to them is, "*You can do this*, and it is within your power."

We would meet at 5 a.m. during the week and at 8 a.m. on Saturdays in front of my *ShapelyGirl* fitness center, a haven for all women to come and not feel judged or shamed because of their size or weight. The physical training was the easy part; it was the mental challenge to look deeper inside and push aside any inhibitions they were harboring inside that was the hard part. I stressed to them that running long distances would take a tremendous toll on their body, and no one backed out. I was ecstatic for them and their tenacity, when so many might have given up. I wanted them to believe in themselves, which meant I needed them to realize that their rational skills were what they needed to overcome the physical challenges they would face before the finish line.

Their minds would either be an asset to push them beyond limits or drag them down into a cesspool of negative emotions. I communicated to them over and over, "As you run past the volunteers on the streets, grab a cup of water and envision the water as a cup of energy, motivation, and success. As you drink, feel the cool water reaching the cells of your body." I needed everyone, including myself, to visualize our bodies gaining strength in all the muscles and joints as we propelled ourselves forward.

Personally, I have done all I can to make it to the end. I physically trained, ate proper nutrition, worked on my visual and motivation skills, and rested. Now I am ready. I need to create that rhythm to carry me down Broad Street along with the other runners and walkers, who are all moving toward the finish line. Some want to win, but, like me, most just want to finish. As I stand among the crowd, it is time to create that rhythm and go with it, for this will be a long journey. One little negative thought can take me away from the goal I can already see in front of me. I not only need the sounds of the music and my positive thinking to take me to the end, but I have to get into prayer for angels to put wings on my sneakers to lift me when I feel I might physically fall. I feel myself beginning to surge. I've broken through the wall that runners talk about. "Ah, ha, ha, ha, stayin' alive…"

I am at the back of the pack when the gun goes off, and I am ready. It is time to just do it. As the excitement takes over, I create a special rhythm in my head to carry me along. Today it's the Bee Gees. "Whether you're a brother or whether you're a mother, you're stayin' alive, stayin' alive." My pace is great so far. This is the key to my success: keeping my pace and rhythm in sink. "Feel the city breakin' and everybody shakin' and were stayin' alive, stayin' alive." Close to five miles to go. Can I do this? I have done it for the past ten years. What is to stop me now? Only me.

As I approach City Hall, I look up and see the statue of Ben Franklin. I am almost at the half-way marker and can taste success. This is the sixth time I have run this route, and it takes me through different neighborhoods, each with their own customs, culture, and characteristics. As we head south, we move toward my neck of town, the area I know best and grew up in, where I was born and raised, attended elementary through high school, and learned that the only comfort was eating.

These streets had been my home ever since I could remember, since the time I was a lonely, little, fat girl who would eat a gallon of ice cream waiting for my mother to come home from work. I had lived all over this neighborhood and began to see and hear the cheers from the crowds ahead. Soon, I hear my name called. This is my part of town, and the comfort I feel on these streets also helps power me to put one foot in front of the other. I can feel success.

I remember my mother being absent both physically and emotionally most of the time. She once told me that if abortions were legal, she would have aborted me. I am sure she said it out of anger and did not mean it, but her words pierced my heart and landed deep inside. This emotional hurt could only be relieved by a binge that would numb me and ease the pain. At her funeral, with her friends and family there, I remember fighting the confusion and bitterness. "Why couldn't you protect me, Mom?"

When I see La Rosa's pizzeria, I am only a few miles away from the finish. This is what I have worked for over the past months with team *ShapelyGirl*. Now, I not only see but taste victory. I am now entrenched in motivational self-talk to get me to my goal. Along the way, I have stayed hydrated because the Philly humidity is brutal and staying hydrated is vital. As I finish, I am wondering where my team is. We trained physically and mentally to cheer each other on as a connected sisterhood. Together, we would help each other finish the race.

It was not about our time but the victory of finishing that we each tasted. We did it, and that was sweet. This group of plus-size women was so close to my heart. We passed the sports stadiums, home of the Eagles and Phillies, and FDR

Park, where I love to run in the morning with my adorable yellow lab, Hannah. It is also the place where I've been taking my *ShapelyGirl* team to train.

Over thirty years ago, at three-hundred-plus pounds, there was no one to show me the way out; to show me that I could learn to move my body and that moving and breathing would feel so good. There was no one to tell me that the abuse I experienced in childhood wasn't my fault and that I did not need to drag that heavy burden with me throughout my life. I discovered on my own that moving my body, breathing, and sweating would finally enable me to let go of the overwhelming feeling of sadness that I carried with me virtually every second of my first twenty-five years.

I lost 150 pounds and found my way to good health. This is what I so dearly wish for all those I train in *ShapelyGirl*. I want them to feel how fabulous good health is. This thought drives me as I see the finish line ahead. The crowd lining both sides of Broad Street is cheering now. We're across. *We are less than one mile away.* I'm behind the finish line, scanning the runners still racing for our signature pink *ShapelyGirl* T-shirts.

Six of my team members have already completed the course, but I'm nervously waiting for my other four girls. To a lot of people, most of my team might look like those who have little interest in an athletic event requiring this level of fitness and commitment. But I know two things: The training will see them to the end, and it will mean everything to them.

The elite runners completed the race almost an hour and a half ago. For the runners crossing the finish line now, it's a question of personal best and a sense of accomplishment. I want that for my team. They worked so hard! With two minutes left on the clock, as the police prepare to remove the metal barricades that keep cars and pedestrians off Broad Street, I spot a flash of hot pink in the crowd. It is the rest of my team, drenched with sweat, faces red, but they can see the finish line. My entire *ShapelyGirl* team is screaming and jumping up and down as the rest of their team crosses the finish line. For these women, I'm optimistic that this could spark a new way of thinking about themselves and what they are capable of. It's all about finding the courage to take that first step.

Team *ShapelyGirl* has opened the refreshment bags all the runners get after the race. They are drinking their bottles of vitamin water and eating the dried fruit. In a few minutes, we'll all head home to shower and change. Then we will enjoy a celebration lunch at Marra's, one of my all-time favorite restaurants. This is a good moment, and I can tell my team of curvy athletes is feeling it too.

Along with a sense of accomplishment, I realize I have a larger mission ahead. I want to reach out to women everywhere to tell them, "It's okay to face the trauma you have suffered in your life. I want you to understand that you don't have to eat to dull the pain. You can find safety and self-comfort in healthy ways." Teaching women about nutrition and fitness isn't enough. Dieting is not a solution. This race we call life is also a mental game. We need the mental skills to stop punishing ourselves with compulsive eating. We must find forgiveness for ourselves and those who wronged us.

I have been on a life journey for over thirty-five years and have grown in so many ways.

- I have learned to love myself just as I am, with all my imperfections.
- I have learned to feel my emotions and not eat because of them. In fact, that is probably my biggest accomplishment to date.

- I have learned to let go of negative emotions and move on.
- I have learned to deal with my problems, especially the ones I cannot control.
- I have learned to stand up for myself — and for me, that is a major component of not binging.
- I have learned that what people do or say has no power over me. The power is in how I handle it.

I went from a broken, obese woman with a full-blown food addiction to a dedicated athlete with a master's degree in sports psychology. I teach other women what I know about making lasting change. However, working with these women has shown me that it is nearly impossible for them to lose weight and get fit if they have unaddressed issues of abuse in their background.

Researchers have started to document what I already know to be true: There is a connection between trauma and obesity. In our society, when someone sees an anorexic, they say, "She really needs treatment." When they see a four-hundred-pound woman, they say, "Wow, she really needs to go on a diet." Binge Eating Disorder isn't even fully recognized by the Diagnostic and Statistical Manual of Mental Disorders (DSM-5). We can't wait for the scientists and the medical profession to figure this out.

I pack my running gear in the trunk of my car. The Broad Street Run is over for today, and now I embark on a new pursuit. I am ready to tell my story in the hope that I will show other women that they're not alone. It's time to share my secrets, and I will invite other *ShapelyGirls* to do the same. We're all part of a great circle of women.

Many of us have experienced trauma, blamed ourselves, and kept quiet for much too long. By telling our stories and discovering our common experience, our broken pieces can come back together again. I hope that by reading my story, other women who have also remained silent will find a path to speak their truth and find healing.

# He Would Whisper

*My first sexual trauma came when I was almost fifteen years old. I was date raped. After that I got into an abusive relationship. For years, I could not talk about it, but now I can. There are times when certain sounds and smells can bring back something traumatic, and it's difficult for a moment. When I was younger, it wasn't safe to talk about it. My mom and my family would assume everything was my fault. They would call me names. Because of that, I kept things to myself, turning to food that comforted me, because food didn't judge you. Of course, you've got the added element that the bigger you get the less attention men pay to you. I always felt it was easier to be called a "fat ass" than have someone grab my breasts when I didn't want them to.*

*— Nadine*

*M*y mother and I sit in a therapy session. She tells the therapist what a happy childhood I have had. Why did I drag her to a therapy session when there is nothing wrong? She does not get it! I guess she was oblivious to the fact that I was over one-hundred-pounds overweight during my happy childhood. Every day, I devoured so much food, on some level I must have believed the binging would bury the shameful secrets I kept from everyone. I had thought this therapy session would lighten my emotional load; instead, it weighed on me for years. I had no vision for my future and not one positive goal for my life. I desperately wanted things to be better but was so stuck in my pain that I couldn't see how I'd ever take control of my own destiny.

That dark place was so different from where I exist now! I sometimes must ask myself, "Did all that really happen?" Yes, it did really happen; but I found my way out. I worked hard and now have a career where I try to be an inspiration to other women who feel immobilized by obesity, shame, and depression.

The way out of a dark place begins by seeing it for what it is.

My mother could be very distant, cold, and controlling. Around others and in public she always seemed a bubbly, happy, cheery woman, who showed no signs of stress in her life. She was the mom making cookies in the kitchen. However, in private she was moody, with all signs pointing to me, as if was my fault. At home, she could and would give me the cold shoulder by rarely speaking to me. She was pre-occupied with her life.

I guess not all was a loss. What she lacked in emotion she made up in keeping a roof over my head. I truly wish I had had a better relationship with her, but sadly, that was not how it ended. When she died, I was very sorry things were not better between us. I never blamed myself, but for a long time I wondered if I had tried hard enough. Was I patient enough with her? She just could not grasp my reality, or perhaps I never saw hers.

Since my mother was a single parent and worked a lot, I spent most of my childhood at my grandparents'. Joe and Viola lived in a very small and modest row house with wonderful neighbors. I was always happy to be with them. Any dignity I had about my life was attributed to them. While both my parents were too busy with their own lives, my grandparents loved me unconditionally.

After school, I would run to their house. I always felt loved there. Grandmother Viola would be in her housedress with a bright, sunny apron on, and there was always a pot of something cooking on the stove. She would stop what she was doing and sit with me. We would talk about things over tea and her favorite tea biscuits, always with margarine. When my period started, I was with her. She took me to the store and explained what was happening to my body. She explained what I needed to buy, wear, and how to use it. She taught me that women who got their periods could get pregnant. I was eleven years old.

While my grandfather loved me with an indifference to my fatness, my grandmother desperately wanted me to lose weight, and I wanted to do it for her. I remember the day she told me how proud of me she was for losing weight and how great I looked. She always complimented me. Those words still ring in my heart when I think of her. She was a woman with love in her soul.

When the time came, she would say to me, "It is time for your grandfather to come home." I was so excited to see him! I would sit on the front steps with Jody, the little, white poodle they bought me. Both Jody and I loved my grandfather. When he would come around the corner, it was a race to see who could run faster, me or Jodie. Jodie always won but, in my eyes, I had the bigger prize, the love of my grandpop, who made me feel safe and secure.

Grandpop would kiss me all over. In his eyes, I was a rock star. He doted on me. I was his pride and joy, no matter how big I was. I have the happiest memories of my life with him. He would take me horseback riding every week. I rode the same pony, and he told me he bought her just for me. I believed him. I loved that pony and wanted to take her home. I named her Sheekie, and we would always have ice cream after our visit with my pony.

My grandfather took me to the shore and the boardwalk, and he would always take some of my girlfriends from Mole Street. We even went to Florida, just the two of us. He belonged to the Cement Masons Union, and every week he would put on his suit and hat to play cards with the guys. He loved playing cards and told me that one day, we would take a long vacation just the two of us.

I remember the smell of his cologne. He always told me that one day, he would dance at my wedding in his suit and tie. I loved being with him, so when he died he took part of my heart with him. I was fifteen years old. I still have wonderful memories of life with him and my grandmother. They were the rock and stability I needed. I loved them more than words could explain.

Life in my mother's house was in sharp contrast to being cherished and safe. I believe that deep down inside my mother's soul, she knew what was going on. She let it go on for years. How could she not know? When I entered therapy many years later, the memories were hard to face. I remember her shadow as she walked past the room my brother and I shared in that tiny house on Iseminger Street in south Philly. I see it like it happened yesterday.

The memory of what my mother allowed to happen to me has never left me. I wanted to cry out to her for help, but instead I would lay there and just do what he wanted. She gave him her blessing. She threw me to him to protect herself from any intimacy or sex he needed. Why would she not protect me? He told me she said it was okay, but I was never to tell her or she would be mad at me. Since she brought him into our house as a supposed father figure, I was afraid he would leave us, and she would be angry with me. So, I just shut up.

My brother and I had bunk beds. I am pretty sure he was on the top bunk most of the time when the abuse happened, but we never spoke about it. It was just my mother's and my unspoken secret. She never gave me the maternal love I needed. That was the hardest issue to address and come to terms with in my therapy sessions. The woman who was supposed to love, protect, and keep me from harm did none of that.

My mother guarded her heart and emotions like the walls of Jericho. Most of the time, she would push me away from her. I really believe she had a disdain for me. She was more consumed with her life, and whatever she did for me she did out of duty. Her relationship with my father never amounted to any security or financial stability for her. She would tell me over and over that she never received any support from him. My grandparents picked up that responsibility. Many times, I tried to get close to her on a deep level, even when all the secrets surfaced and the confrontations came pouring out at our family meeting. I believe she would have had a meltdown if she had not kept her cool.

Joe and Viola were my rock. If not for them, I am sure I would have not survived the trauma of those early years.

They were always there for me, but I never said a word to them about what was going on in my house; after all, they even loved my abuser, as he kept a roof over our heads. Who would believe me? I kept my mouth shut and ate to hide the pain.

My father left us early on, and I guess my mother was forced into a life she wasn't prepared for. I am not aware that my mother suffered any abuse, but there were hints that something happened to her in her past, secrets she never talked about. She was a very beautiful woman, and that was her ticket. She worked as a waitress, but the money she earned was never enough. For my mother, it was always about the money. The easiest way out was to manipulate men to provide for us.

After she divorced my father, she met a guy at a bakery. Marsh was a numbers writer or bookie, as they were called in those days. He ran illegal gambling, and the money just flowed. This was her ticket to financial freedom. She bought a beach house. We went on vacations. At Christmastime, we had lots of gifts. She took me to the malls every week to buy, buy, buy. The sad part was that I had almost no emotional connection with her, and that bothered me. It was not until I left home and was gone for years that she said, "I love you." Did she mean it? I wanted to believe she did.

The only man my mother ever really loved was Clint. He was one of her customers at a restaurant where she worked, and they hit it off. She started to see him and told me about this affair with him a year later. I was the only one who knew her secret. She worshipped him, and he did her. He was a man's man and treated my mother like a queen. Clint lavished her with gifts and overnight trips. He was a very sophisticated guy, and you could tell from the way they looked at each other that they were madly in love.

I asked her once, "Why aren't you guys together?" She told me he was married. He was a businessman, who was very wealthy but had a sick wife he would never leave. His wife had Parkinson's disease and was in a wheelchair. He made the terms of the relationship clear to my mother, and she seemed to be okay with that. He was a big part of our lives when I was growing up, but it was another secret we never discussed.

Normally, my mother went out with Clint on Mondays and Fridays and Saturday during the day. He always drove a big, shiny, new white Cadillac with red interior. I would get in and could smell the freshness of the new leather. Mom and I hit the big times. Money was no object, and I went with them to the best restaurants money could buy. We were dining at places like Le Bec Fin. Sometimes, they would take me to motels and I would sit in the car and wait for them while they were inside. If I was with her, nobody could question where she'd been or what she was doing. I was her loyal alibi, and so I was pulled into her web of secrets and lies.

My mother would leave us with her boyfriend, Marsh, while she went out with Clint. She was Marsh's caretaker. He never got a license or drove a car. She told him what to wear, what to eat, what time to get up, and where to go. He was an immature man-child, who lived with his mother but spent most days at our house. Late at night, he would take a cab home, or his friend Smitty would pick him up.

Marsh was there most Saturday afternoons. I think he thought she was working, but he never questioned her comings or goings. The anxiety would build inside me, knowing what was coming. Marsh was repulsive. He smelled like old tobacco. He smoked these big, fat cigars and was always touching himself. He was the kind of guy you'd see in a peep show, and sometimes he made inappropriate comments in front of us. I was terrified to be alone with him. I was about eight years old and completely vulnerable. There was nobody to protect me. No mother, no father, no one. She left me and my younger brother alone with him.

I don't know exactly when the abuse started, but I remember to his day very vividly what happened. We lived in a small, two-bedroom row house. Because I was older and bigger, I was on the bottom bunk in the bedroom I shared with my brother. Our bunk beds were against the wall. As I said before, I am sure my mother was there many times, as I remember seeing her shadow through the crack under the bedroom door while Marsh was in my bed.

He would come into the bedroom, shut the door, and ask me if I wanted a backrub. I was afraid to say no, for fear he would leave and my mother would be angry. Instinctively, I turned on my left side, facing the wall. The room was very quiet, and he would lie down and whisper in my right ear, often asking me if I had started my period yet. To this day, I sometimes get horrible earaches in my right ear.

If I turned to answer him, he would turn my head back to the wall, so I wasn't facing him. He was never clean shaven and had whiskers. I think he was afraid he would chafe my face and someone would find out what he was doing. After rubbing my back, he would then begin the sickening ritual of touching me inappropriately and eventually raping me. He did all this from behind, so he was sure not to look at me. When he was finished, he'd tell me not to move while he cleaned me with a wash cloth. Then he'd go out to the living room and smoke a cigar.

It was the same scenario time after time. It continued until I was about eleven years old. He probably stopped because I had started my period and he didn't want me to get pregnant. My brother and I never talked about this, but I

do have a memory of my brother being on those bunk beds, possibly while I was being abused.
My heart and soul were broken.

> *It's a scary feeling but I will try my hardest. My life has been such a mess, but the support is here. The new therapist is Frank, and I like him a lot. Everything is complicated, but it will work out. I think of my parents but cannot see them. I will never speak to my dad but hope my mom is ok. My being molested as a child has not bothered me, so I will deal with it at later time.*
>
> *Excerpt from my journal —*
> *January 10, 1990*

You don't always know when a child has been sexually abused. The abuse occurs in secret and most times will leave no physical scars; however, most children experience anxiety, suicidal thoughts, and other symptoms of Post-Traumatic Stress Disorder (PTSD). They may also act out their trauma with behaviors ranging from aggression and delinquency to precocious sexual behavior, hyperactivity, and addiction. Some kids go through their daily lives without anyone recognizing the damage that has been inflicted on them. I did not act out as a kid, but I began eating compulsively to escape reality and numb my feelings. The only noticeable symptom I displayed was my fat body.

The whispers of a vile monster caused me to begin eating my secrets.

# 3

# A Pound of Bacon and Boxes of Mac and Cheese

As an Italian woman, I especially know that food represents love. Eating is usually the center of family gatherings. Whether it's birthday cake, a turkey and dressing holiday, or Sunday pasta day, we use food to symbolize love. Food used for comfort, such as chili, meatloaf, apple pie, mashed potatoes, ice cream, and macaroni and cheese, are staples we associate with Mom's home cooking, family dinners, and good times with friends. These foods are appealing because their fatty, sugary, and savory flavors give us a sense of satisfaction and well-being. Most of us eat these foods occasionally, but restaurants center their menus around comfort foods. For many of us, food and eating replaces real love and affection, attention, and comfort. The revolving door to achieve this level of pleasure and security consists of compulsive dieting, starving, overeating, binging, and eating disorders.

Those who have studied eating and the brain have found that after consuming an excessive amount of fatty, sugary foods, our bodies produce opioids — the same chemical substance that makes drug addicts feel good after taking heroin or cocaine. Scientists call these "palatable" foods, a combination of sugar, fat, and salt that appeal to the reward center of the brain.

Mental health professionals used to think that emotional and behavioral problems associated with children who suffered abuse were primarily the result of psychological damage. The treatment was talk therapy, or they were expected to "get over it." More recent investigations into the aftermath of trauma paints a different picture. Because child abuse takes place at a critical time, when the brain is still being shaped, severe mistreatment can leave a kind of a scar. Trauma changes the neurobiology of the brain.

These changes also help explain why some people are unable to shake off negative experiences in their past and are more likely to become addicted to food and other substances. When scientists at McGill University conducted autopsies on people who had been abused and neglected in childhood and went on to commit suicide, they found their brains to be much more biologically vulnerable to stress. (From the *Journal Nature Neuroscience*, February 2009.) When we are traumatized physically or emotionally, our brains respond by secreting cortisol, the hormone that alerts the body to stress. The brain has receptors, whose job is to clear the cortisol and protect the brain's neurons from prolonged exposure.

Overweight or obese women with a history of trauma are quick to blame themselves for failing at weight loss. They see themselves as weak-willed human beings. We need to understand the biological battles our bodies are fighting after experiencing trauma. For instance, we now know that abuse disrupts the hormonal system involved in metabolism and the way fat is deposited in the body. The hormone cortisol has been identified as a major player in this process, and over-weight people have higher levels of cortisol than thinner peo-ple. Not only does cortisol elevate blood sugar and increase hunger, but also it raises blood pressure and suppresses the immune system. It is not hard to see how these factors would result in someone developing the much-talked-about met-abolic syndrome that leads to diabetes, heart disease, and stroke. Cortisol is also responsible for fat deposits around the center of the body.

A recent study compared women who gain weight mostly around the belly with women who tend to gain weight around the hips. The women with more abdominal fat had higher cortisol levels. They reported that they felt more overwhelmed by demanding tasks and had much more difficulty in handling stress. The long-term effects of sexual abuse can include low self-esteem and poor body image as well as a lack of impulse control, promiscuity disorder, and drug abuse. All these factors contribute to binge eating and subsequent obesity.

Looking back, I see how I was destined to be obese. My family and I were clueless about the connection of trauma to compulsive eating. My family thought I lacked self-control; I thought food was my savior. Early on, I became a binge eater.

My mother would tell my brother and me, "I'm going out for a couple of hours." We knew what that meant: We would not see her until dinnertime. That left me to watch my younger brother all day. However, when I heard the door close, I didn't care. It was time for my weekly food orgy. Time to be alone with food. For this reason, I looked forward to her going almost every Saturday.

I was happy that no one could bother me as I got ready for my food fest, my time to escape my misery for a while. My brother was content watching cartoons. He was so engrossed in the TV, he would never bother me. That made it more special. No interruptions. I had to have my food fix! Food was my friend, my comfort that allowed me to suppress the pain stirring within me. I had a celebration and rituals with food. I was a raging food addict on a vacation!

Living in South Philly, I would run to Cacia's Italian Bakery, located on the corner of my grandparent's narrow street. I would get the largest hoagie rolls, hot out of the brick stone oven. They were long and crusty, begging me to take them home to enjoy. My mother always kept a lot of food in the fridge, and since I especially loved bacon, she would buy pounds of it. If a pound or so was missing in a day, she would never notice, right?

Week after week this ceremonial ritual consisted of me lining up the food: hot rolls, Hellman's mayonnaise, and a whole package of bacon. I would open the package, take one bacon strip at a time and lay them in the pan so that all strips would cook crispy. Not only can I remember the sound of the bacon sizzling while it fried, but the smell was magical. I was in a state of pure ecstasy and would salivate like a dog.

I was in Heaven as I made the sandwiches and Kraft macaroni and cheese. I would devour at least one box and sometimes two. Along with the bacon, I used gobs of mayonnaise and spread it all over the bread. Nothing else mattered but bacon, mayonnaise, fresh hoagie rolls, and mac and cheese. The house could be on fire, and I probably would not have noticed. Today, when I eat or smell bacon, I sometimes go back to those days.

As a young girl, this was my world. I guess you could say that my mother and I were co-dependent. She let me eat, and I let her use me. What a perfect set-up. It worked for both of us. My mother never asked me about what or how much I ate. Surely, she noticed the food was missing; however, it was like a magic trick. The food was there, and then it was gone. She never seemed curious about its disappearance, and I never offered to tell her. She never talked about my weight. The size of my body was never an issue with her. She just let me do my thing in shame, the same way she did hers in secret.

I never divulged any of this to anyone. I kept my mother's and my sinister secrets to myself. I did this because she asked me to and because her silence about my secret sins allowed me to continue in them. We kept each other's secrets. While my brother never knew where she was going, I knew she was going to meet Clint.

Clint lavished her with beautiful jewelry and a home at the beach. When I graduated high school, my mother took eight of us to Hawaii, and on the second day at the beach, there was Clint, staying at the same hotel as the rest of us. I was the distraction she needed to get away with Clint and ensure that Marsh, the boyfriend she had a love-hate relationship with, would not suspect. Marsh was the other sugar daddy keeping us out of poverty. He was happy to pay the bills and be my mother's puppet. He obliged her like a puppy waiting for its treats.

I can only imagine how her life would have been different had Clint been single, but he was not. Some years later, Clint became ill with cancer. I can still hear her voice cracking as she told me he was in the hospital and very sick. I stood by and watched my mother, heartbroken over this man she truly loved. She was there when he took his last breath. We both cried. I felt such sorrow and compassion for my mother. I felt a real connection with her at that moment.

Later in my life, as I began to run emotional eating groups and do fitness coaching with women, the stories poured out about their mothers confronting them about their eating. Most of the women would always divulge how their mothers nagged and subjected them to ridicule. My experience was the opposite; my mother avoided any conversation about food or eating. She never asked where the food had gone, what I did, or what I ate all day. If I ate three pounds of M&M's or the fridge was empty just days after a trip to the grocery, she never said a word. This led me to believe she didn't care.

The little girl inside me knew her mother was only worried about her own life and didn't care about her child's. If she had, she would have addressed my eating and weight early on. I am sure her pathetic reasoning was, "If she wants to be fat, leave her alone." While most of my aunts, great aunts, and grandmothers watched every morsel that passed my lips, my mother remained mute. Even at family dinners. I could gorge and eat as much as I wanted while she sat in silence. She let everyone else do the dirty work to make me feel even worse. I wonder why? We never went to *Weight Watchers* or any other diet program; instead, she left the nagging to my grandmother, who tried to get me to lose weight daily.

My grandmother was always addressing my weight. Even though I saw it as nagging, I knew it was out of love for me. She wanted me to be normal in a world that hated fat girls. When my father was around, she had him drag me to every diet doctor in the area. It was very uncomfortable for both of us, and nothing helped. It would be years before I was finally ready to face myself and get clean and sober about food.

# Gere

I met Gere at St. Maria Goretti High School. It was our first day, and we sat across from each other in the cafeteria. We were two giddy fourteen-year-olds, looking forward to this journey of entering womanhood. We were so excited and could not contain our enthusiasm that we were now freshmen in high school. We talked and laughed for what seemed hours, and I felt connected to her; but I was not sure why. It was almost miraculous that we became friends.

High school would not give me the opportunity to meet other girls my age. All the Catholic parish students in the area streamed into one high school. I would leave my neighborhood every day and venture into unknown territory. Consequently, I kept the friends I already had instead of acquiring new ones. As I looked around the cafeteria, my new home for the next four years, I dreamed of getting thin, having a boyfriend, and falling in love. I had none of those things. I was fat, boys did not like me, and I knew nothing about love.

High school was the time most girls talked about college. Even though I did well in elementary school, I never thought I would be college material. I was surviving in a world with no hope. I had no dreams or vision of what my future looked like. College never entered my mind. Only smart girls went to college, not fat ones who thought about eating all day. Not girls who could not control their lives and kept horrible secrets. And certainly, not a girl whose mother was divorced and ostracized from the Catholic Church.

By sixth grade, I was the tallest and biggest girl in my class. One other girl was tall, and I remember we always were sent to the back of the line when we needed to line up. In high school, I noticed girls who were taller than me and some overweight girls, but not many. The tall ones were the athletes, the pretty ones were going to college, and the popular ones were red-ribbon girls. I was none of those. I was fat and tall. I saw myself as an ugly duckling in a sea of swans.

Gere was not overweight and ate very little. She had lots of boyfriends. Her dress size was a single digit, and she was stunning. She was vibrant, artsy, pretty, and curvy. She came from St. Thomas Parish, on the other side of town. I was from St. Monica, and we were from two different worlds; but we found each other in this mob of ninth graders. We were drawn together in a peculiar way I did not understand.

Between our girly giggles, Gere and I found out we had the same birthday, March 16th. We screamed and hugged each other like we both won an Oscar. We were born on the same day, at the same hospital, and we fantasized that our mothers were roommates in St. Agnes Hospital. To this day, I still believe that. Gere believed the stars lined up and we were to meet because the Earth deemed it. She believed Mother Earth dictated our lives and the Zodiac was our path. I, on the other hand, was not that sure.

To ensure our friendship forever, we decided to do the pinky ritual. This would make us blood sisters for sure. We pricked our pinky fingers and then put our fingers together, mingling our blood. This confirmed that no one could come between us. Our friendship was sealed. This was the start of our lifelong connection for the next forty-five years.

Gere and I hung out through high school, even though I was a compulsive eater and she never let food dictate her life. She lived and dreamed out of the box and wanted to be a shrink or an actress. She was artistic, and in tenth grade she wanted to try out for the Bishop Neumann play Mr. Perry directed. It was an honor and a big deal to audition and get picked. This is how all future stars got to Hollywood, or so they thought. Gere was no different. By then she wanted to be an actress or punk rock star. She begged me to audition with her.

At first, I said no; but eventually, I gave in. I needed to support her. She was thrilled, and we celebrated with ice cream. She never ate hers, but I finished mine and then hers. The day of the auditions for *Fiddler on the Roof,* I went kicking and screaming. Gere wanted a lead role; I just wanted it to be over. I told her she owed me after this.

She was called in first and came out crying. The stress and anxiety had gotten to her, and she was a mess. I calmed her down and told her they loved her and that she could be an actress, that she was that good. She believed me. They called my name, and in I went.

The room was enormous, and the stage was even bigger. I was sweating, and at one point I wanted to pee myself. I began to joke with the crew, and that was the ice breaker that relaxed me. My thighs were running together. I was wearing my fat clothes, army and navy men's dungarees, a men's purple, long-sleeve pullover with buttons, and a long gold chain with a seven-inch Italian fish with scales dangling down my chest. That was what Italians believed was good luck when I was a kid: a fish with scales on it.

I was so nervous, I thought I would faint. I kept thinking, *I am going to kill Gere for making me do this.* But it became easier when I realized she would have done the same for me. I had to sing, "Sunrise, Sunset," and I was terrible. I could not carry a tune, and my voice cracked the whole time. I made jokes and laughed at myself, and they seemed to be amused. By the end of the audition, I was in tears. I felt so humiliated. I was fat and sweating. I could feel a binge coming on. Gere would join me, even though she never ate.

They told us we would hear from them in two weeks. I completely forgot about it until the letters came. Gere called me, crying that she was rejected. What? But she was going to be a Hollywood actress! How could they not see it? I felt terrible for her. So, I threw my letter in the trash. She asked me if I had opened it, and I said, "No. Why should I?" She wanted to know what my letter said. I told her okay.

As I read the letter, I began to cry. I had been chosen for the chorus. How could this be? I couldn't even carry a tune! They must have made a mistake, but they did not. I went to talk to Mr. Perry, and he explained that I had the personality he was looking for. He said I was the ice breaker for the show. Ice breaker? What did that mean? He put me in the back of the chorus and asked me to mimic singing, and I did.

So, I became the ice breaker for future stars who were uptight and wanted to go to Hollywood. I wanted to give Gere my letter, but that never happened, and we worked through it. We never talked about it until many years later. As a friend, l loved her like a sister; she was my go-to girl for any deep conversations about life. As Gere and I got older, I told her about the abuse, and she confided that her grandfather had abused her. She told me he would repeatedly force his tongue in her mouth. We both laughed and thought it was disgusting. In my craziness, I thought, *At least my abuser was not a blood relative.* That made me feel better.

I was pretty well liked in high school, although I was the problem child as I entered tenth grade. I began acting out and got in a lot of trouble. When I met Gere's family, I wanted them to be my family. I fell in love with her parents, Mike and Marie. I wanted her mother to be my mother. Marie was always there for her kids. They were not perfect, but it was the family I never had. Marie always wanted to feed me, and I loved her cooking. Mike and Marie were married until they both died, and I loved Gere's sisters, whom I keep in touch with today.

After high school, Gere went to college, and I was off to see the world. We did not see each other for years, but the bond we shared would never be broken. She moved to New York to marry a hot Argentina baker, whom she deeply loved. She had two sons, while I was trying to deal with my past.

When Gere got divorced and moved back to Philly, we connected again. By then, her boys were becoming teens and she had decided to go to nursing school. She worked hard, day and night, and finally became a nurse. For the next twenty years, she dedicated her life to helping others. When we reconnected in Philly, she told me she had begun to eat to comfort herself. Raising two sons alone was difficult. We talked in depth about food and our relationship with eating. It was clear to me that she was eating out of stress and emotions. She had gained a lot of weight, and her life was a mess.

I spent a lot of time with her while she was in nursing school, and after she graduated, she moved herself and the boys to New Jersey. She bought her first house, and we were both excited. Food was still an issue, but she said her weight never bothered her. I didn't believe her, but I never made an issue out of it. She was my soul sister.

Gere ate compulsively and was a binge eater. She ate her feelings away. Food was her comfort when the world seemed too stressful. We talked very openly about it, as we both had the same issues. She knew that life was hard, and she ate to spite it. We would talk about it, and she would tell me that food was all she wanted for now. I knew that feeling, oh, so well! By this time, I had lost weight and life was different for me. I was into fitness and eating healthy, and Gere was working crazy hours. We talked often and got together when we could. Her weight began to escalate, and I was worried about her health. I was willing to help her, but she was not interested. I decided to let it be. She knew I was there if she wanted my help.

Gere and I celebrated our birthday every year together, either via phone or in person. As we approached our 60th birthday, we decided to go to the Adirondacks to celebrate, just the two of us. We talked about this plan the summer before, and I was looking forward to the trip; but she died five months before our 60th birthday.

I was devastated. I was with her toward the end of her life, and the day she died, part of my soul went with her. I cried over her death more than my own mother's. I think about her and miss her every day. The friendship I shared with her was so special, and it will never be replaced. I know she is with me when I look at the sun, the light of our world. She was the light in my very dark world for a long time, a friend with whom I could share my secrets and not be judged.

# Cycle of Secrecy, Comfort, and Shame

*My father mentally, physically, and sexually abused me. He was not my biological father. His name is on my birth certificate, and he raised me from birth. He was an alcoholic. The abuse began with a grooming process, where he would touch me and then warn me not to tell. When I didn't tell, the touching would escalate. Whenever we were home alone, he was fondling me. He made me touch him. He was having full intercourse with me by age ten. He was violent sometimes and would hit me with a belt. I lived in fear all the time. He would watch me constantly and make comments about the way I looked. I remember summers swimming in the backyard. I felt dirty because he would make inappropriate*

*comments about how sexy I looked in my
bathing suit. I was supposed to be his little
girl. He was sick, but to me still my father.
He would assault me when he felt like it. I
began to binge, and I let my weight escalate
to over 250 pounds.*

— *Sherdina*

*W*hen kids are sexually abused, they are told not to tell,
so we just listen. The shame, stress, and secrets we live
with are too familiar to those of us who have survived sexual
abuse. We become experts at keeping secrets. Abuse victims
sometimes believe they provoked the abuse and internalize
the shame that follows. I always blamed myself for what happened with Marsh, so shame became a huge part of my life
in my younger years.

Shame is carried inside us for a long time. For those
without support, it becomes who we are. We become even
more shamefully entrenched when our eating gets out of control. Many survivors begin to engage in behaviors that rein-
force their shame, like binge eating, alcoholism, promiscuity,
and drug abuse. I became entrenched in the thought that
the abuse was my fault, which surfaced as toxic shame and
blocked my ability to become a healthy, productive adult.

Secret eating is a marker for Binge Eating Disorder
(BED). You eat alone out of anxiety and depression. The eating is pleasurable for a time but is quickly followed by feelings
of shame, regret, and self-loathing. The sense of self-disgust
and failure can be unbearable and brings about more depression and anxiety, which triggers more binging. For whatever
reason, not telling anyone forms the prison cell that keeps
the cycle of self-abuse going. It is a conspiracy of silence that

fosters emotional turmoil, presents binging as the remedy, and then shame and self-loathing take root even more.

Binging was time set aside for me and my food. I felt safe, cared for, comforted, and calm. Eating always calmed down the painful and intolerable feelings. I found a secret place to enjoy my food free of embarrassment or interruption. Nobody was there to witness what, how much, or how fast I devoured the food. Nobody could judge me. For me, being alone was a key to full satisfaction.

Feelings about food can take on a sense of intimacy. After all, food is there when everything and everyone else has let you down. It can feel like your best friend. I would often hear women in groups referring to "my food" in a possessive, protective manner. I know I did. This possessiveness created obstacles in our lives.

The ritualistic ways in which some compulsive eaters use food are an attempt to elevate it to something more meaningful. Eating becomes almost sacramental, with the false promise to transform us. Just as the communion host offers God's grace to those who consume it, we see ceremonial eating as the way to receive God's gift of salvation from our suffering.

From a young age, I was aware that overeating was seen as a sign of moral weakness and poor character. According to *Wikipedia*, gluttony is derived from a Latin word that means, "to gulp down or swallow." It is described as overeating and drinking to the point of waste. It is considered by most Christian denominations to be one of the seven deadly sins. The notion that we are sinning as we binge only serves to make us more ashamed and secretive about what we are doing.

There are two kinds of shame: healthy shame and toxic shame. Healthy shame is the feeling we get when we cheat on a test or yell at our kids. It reminds us that we have gone too far, hurt someone, or strayed away from our values. Healthy shame is having a conscience and using it as a moral compass. Toxic shame, like the kind experienced by food addicts, is a devastating emotional state that makes us feel painfully diminished as human beings and destroys our sense of well-being. It is like a poison we carry in our soul twenty-four hours a day, punishment that far outweighs the crime.

Toxic shame can be the result of the judgment and rejection of others or a traumatic event or situation for which we blame ourselves or which has convinced us of our lack of value and worth. It is the constant fear that someone will see us as the horrible person we believe we are. Shame convinces us that we are worthless human beings. When we judge ourselves, we binge. When we binge, we judge ourselves. Women who have experienced trauma can have feelings of toxic shame all the time. Even the smallest, negative comment can cause feelings of shame to echo through our deepest selves. Our shame is on auto pilot, and there is no predicting when it might steer us to a place of self-hatred.

Years ago, anytime someone scolded me at work, I took it as a personal attack. It might have been over the smallest issue that needed to be corrected. I was so shame-based from the past that these incidents would devastate me. Instead of just correcting my mistakes, I was paralyzed. This went on for years. I would blame myself and feel inadequate, always believing this was the end. *My secrets have been uncovered, and I will probably be fired. I am so stupid and always mess things up. It's my fault, and he should fire me. I hate myself. I am a terrible person.*

Our shame is a reflection of how we see ourselves, including our bodies. As a compulsive eater, my shame caused me to hate my body. I hated being and feeling fat every day. I hated what I thought my fat body represented. I hated that someone violated me and put me on a negative course. Eating, if only for the moment, would sooth the pain of self-loathing.

Confirming my shame was the stigma of being overweight that is still prevalent in our society. Even moderately overweight women can loathe themselves and feel too ashamed to wear a bathing suit. Prejudice against overweight and obese people has become acceptable in our culture.

Sexual abuse can silence even the loudest voice. Then we have no voice because of our weight. I was silenced during the first abuse that rattled my world. I never felt good enough. I kept quiet. Shame drove me into isolation, silenced my voice, convinced me I was not good enough. When we feel ashamed much of the time, we are less likely to become close to people and risk intimacy. Shame hindered most of my relationships, especially intimate ones.

For a lot of us, we confuse intimacy with sex and never fully understand the difference. I remember thinking that the more sex I had, the more I would find someone to love me. However, I never did grasp the love thing, as I never stayed long enough in a relationship. Every one of my early relationships was chaotic and toxic, and it was always me who bailed out first. I would hurt you before I let you hurt me.

Shame prohibits open, honest communication. It makes us afraid to voice our opinions and is the ugly, critical voice inside our heads that constantly tears us down and reminds us that we are out of control. Shame will keep us captive in our secrets and feeling that we are "bad." I never discussed feeling ashamed with anyone, because it was too painful for me to risk anyone knowing the truth. If they knew me, I might be rejected, and I was not about to feel more abandonment in my life.

A natural response to feeling so much fear of rejection and shame is anger. Years ago, a guy I was dating told me that he grew up in a fatherless home. He was filled with anger and rage. He had no concept of any emotion past the anger. What I saw was a hurt little boy, who did not know how to express what he needed. I have never forgotten that conversation. When we cannot express hurt, we get angry, with the hope of protecting ourselves from more rejection, trauma, and shaming experiences.

Healing from toxic shame required me to take that first step in a non-shaming environment. I had to be able to trust someone and share my secrets, deal with them, and be restored to emotional and physical health. This took time! And the person you trust understands that. For a while, I could only open up a little bit at a time, and knowing that my confidant understood this reduced my anxiety and allowed me to open up more and more. Eventually, I could be fully transparent and deep healing began to take place. Today, my healing is strengthened as I share my life and experience with others, especially those who have had similar life experiences.

People who know you may be shocked to learn that you are suffering from these feelings. They may see you as a wholly loving and capable person. Our brokenness does not always reveal itself on the surface, because we become masters of deception to keep our secrets from being known. Once we share your fears and shame with someone we trust, we can ask for what we need. Instead of living in a shroud of secrets and lies, motivating us to binge and increase our shame, we are strong in the truth that we are loveable, valuable, and capable human beings. Toxic shame is nobody's truth!

The truth destroys the secrets and lies of the past and creates an armor to protect us from the things that trigger toxic shame. It is time to talk about our shame and journal about it. When we understand what we are feeling and what we are afraid of, we can ask for what we need. Then, when people respond to us with love and generosity, we can begin to accept our own worthiness and move closer to freeing ourselves from the patterns of shame that have hurt us for too long.

# 6

# Crushing the Inner Critic

*During my recovery, I did have a massive relapse and began binging for six months. It was then I began to gain back a lot of weight. And now my body is finding its way back and falling into its own place. It's getting better. It's been about a year and a half since I last binged. My binges include eating all the stuff that's supposedly bad for you. I've had to re-define good versus bad. I'm re-learning all the rules and rebelling against all the rules and restrictions my mother placed on me. Sometimes it would be getting a vanilla milkshake every day. Or baking a cake twice a week. My substance was food and I did mimic my parents and their drug addictions.*
— *Serena*

Most of us struggle with demons repeatedly. Positioned in the rational hemisphere of our brain sits that relentlessly powerful, negative voice, letting us know how imperfect we are the minute we do something contrary to social standards: *You are fat. You are a loser. You are a failure. You are a pig. You will never lose weight. You will never be the perfect size.* This evil voice reminds us how flawed we are. For years, it manipulated my thoughts, leading me to believe that I was awful because I was fat. Again, I hated being fat every day. I hated to look at my body, which confirmed my failure and loneliness.

And so, I binged. I hid food. I ate out of trash cans. I lied to get food. I ate until I could not breathe. I ate to get rid of the pain that encompassed me. Even though my body was surrounded in fat and self-hatred, I continued to binge, praying the pain would subside. I was in pain and denial, and not dealing with my pain hindered my relief. I did not know how to overcome it; but for the moment, eating helped.

Early on, I resigned myself to a life of yo-yo dieting, counting every calorie, diet after diet, dancing in an endless cycle of shame, guilt, and resentment. Every time I ate sugary, caloric, or fattening foods such as cookies, cakes, and candy, I felt like I had committed a crime. I was *bad* for eating cake; I was *good* for eating carrots. I hated myself when I ate candy, but I was the perfect person eating a grapefruit. I let those thoughts of *good* and *bad* devour me. The minute any unhealthy calories passed my lips, that inner critic would declare me a convicted felon.

The inner critic enforces the moral standards of good and bad on our eating habits. It lays down the law: "You are not allowed to eat this! You cannot even think about that!" Everything my inner critic says causes a downward spiral in my brain of complete self-loathing, self-criticism, and self-hatred. Sound familiar? You too?

It might only take one bite or after hundreds of calories being consumed, but we tell ourselves how *bad* we are. Where did we learn such hatred towards ourselves? Who taught us that even a morsel of food could wreak such havoc within us? Why did we allow this inner critic to reside in us and destroy any belief that we were an amazing creature? And how do we break free of the inner critic?

We are human beings with many flaws, but we have the capacity to make as well as stick to a commitment and step away from self-punishment. We must let go of any instant gratification in exchange for long-term possibilities. It is time to understand our physical impulses and get them under our control, to take a stand against the inner critic. Promising never to binge or overeat again is not putting unnecessary stress on our body, mind, and spirit; but it can be a revolution of change for us. We can't do this apart from coming to realize who we really are and what we can be and do.

The inner critic does not want you to feel any sense of accomplishment or have any positive view of your world. It is there to make you feel like a complete failure and make your head spin with feelings of inadequacy and worthlessness. Did you know that this inner critic is a liar? The truth is, your life is filled with possibilities and wonder. Just look around you and find it! Don't let the inner critic hiss at you like a snake and corner you, making you feel like you have nowhere to go. You are valued and have plenty of places to go!

You need to have a continuous positive conversation with yourself. Say, "I refuse to listen to negativity that has no truth. I am valued today. I am worth it!" After practicing this new habit for a while, in the absence of that toxic voice is a robust, amazing person, capable of what you desire and dare to do. Every time that inner critic begins to speak lies, stop it and remind yourself who you really are. You are powerful, wonderful, and can conquer any negative thought or desire.

Have *that* conversation daily. When the inner critic stirs you up to act on impulse, crush it. You are stronger than you think.

Many of us received this inner critic through our mothers, who have tremendous influence in our lives. What they say and how they behave has an impact on how we look at the world and see ourselves, and this worldview shapes our decisions in life. Healthy mothers have innate motherly instincts. They respect our feelings and emotions, love us no matter what, feel our pain and extend a shoulder to cry on when we get dumped by our first love, pick us up when we fall, and cheer us on as we head to college or our first job. We should never fear baring our souls to them, for their love helps to glue the shattered pieces of our lives together.

On the other hand, toxic mothers make us feel ugly, unlovable, and unworthy. With this view of ourselves, we naturally see the world confirming these lies. Toxic mothers can make us feel like we are not good enough as ourselves. We must be skinnier, prettier, smarter, nicer — and we bring all this into every relationship we have, including our relationship with ourselves.

As women, we must understand the impact we have on each other and ourselves. Our sharp, merciless judgments on ourselves can ruin our lives. We make these judgments based on what we heard, saw, and read over the course of our childhood, as well as any trauma we may have suffered. It is very hard to be positive when we grew up with negativity as our anchor. However, we have the capacity to turn that around by understanding our worth and value.

Once I grasped this truth and changed my thinking, I could let go of the past. I learned new tools that worked like gorilla glue to make me whole. Even today, I sometimes have those negative thoughts, but I do not dwell on them, entertain them, or even listen to them. I shut them down and listen to the real me.

As a young woman, I was always in search of a mother figure. She came along when I was in college. I befriended one of my professors, who invited me to the Omega Institute in Rhinebeck, New York, for a weekend. I had wanted to go to the Omega Institute to connect with myself in some way. I was searching for answers and thought that a workshop might help. My professor told me I would not only cleanse my mind but my body as well.

The menu was strictly vegetarian. Could I binge on greens and tofu for three days? I was about to find out! We enrolled in a mother/daughter workshop for the weekend, which was taught by Dorothy and Julie Firman, authors of the book, *Mothers and Daughters.* I wanted to know how I could be a better daughter and get my mother to love me. What was I doing wrong? How would I get her to notice my life?

At the workshop, I met a woman named Andy and her daughter Karen. The workshop was packed with about one hundred women, and somehow this mother/daughter duo and I floated toward each other. As I watched their relationship for three days, it was so apparent that the apple did not fall too far from the tree. They interacted with love, kindness, and compassion toward each other. They were connected, intertwined, and so loving. I wanted that relationship too!

How come I never had that? How could I get it? I wanted my mother to be my best friend not my adversary. I hung out with them for the duration of the workshop. While there, I learned I was not alone in my quest for my mother to engulf me. Woman after woman bore their innermost thoughts about their childhoods. After three emotional days, I discovered that some mothers just lacked the tools of good parenting, such as love, compassion, and understanding. I realized I might not get what I needed from my own mother.

My mother's presence molded a lot of my thinking about myself. She watched me become obese right before her eyes and never said a word. She watched me eat until I could not breathe and acted like this was normal. She knew I was hiding food and remained silent. She was also the opposite of me. She had a passion for buying candy and lots of it; however, I rarely remember her eating it. There would always be bowls of M&M's and Hershey kisses. The only time my mother ate was at the dinner table. She was a sugar lover, and she chose to eat desserts instead of our main course, so there was always plenty to eat for my brother and me.

My mother ridiculed me about friends, what I wore, the makeup I used, and places I went to; but we never discussed my weight. In fact, she pretended I looked like the other girls: skinny. She had convinced herself that I was a good weight because she had to. She instinctively knew my obesity was tied to the sexual abuse. She couldn't deal with my weight without dealing with the abuse. So, she pretended neither existed.

I never remember my mother talking about diets or dieting. She never had to because she had a perfect body and had decided I did too. Not only did she never talk about my body, she never talked about her body. She never criticized herself, and I never saw her weigh herself. She was gorgeous and small, and it wasn't until she got older that she gained any weight.

I have heard story after story from women whose mothers' middle names were diets. Some told me their mothers weighed them almost daily. Some said they were told that men did not like fat women, and they would never get married if they did not stay skinny. For most of my life, my mother looked perfect, and my inner critic used that against me. It screamed, "Go on a diet! Lose this weight!"

Now, I am anti-diet. Any restrictive food program is a diet, and you may take off some weight initially; but if you don't tackle the root problems that are causing you to overeat and binge, you will just gain the weight back. In most cases, you will gain more weight than you lost. You need to learn how to stop listening to the garbage that goes on in your head and rehearse and recite what is true. Every day you can decide to stop listening to the demonic dialogue that perhaps came from a mother who was constantly dieting or criticizing you — or in my case saying nothing, which screamed even louder.

Reject outside influences that promote the message that you are unlovable and subhuman if you are not skinny: movies, commercials, the diet and sometimes the fitness industry. They feed the inner critic. Sometimes our worst moments are when we are out in public to enjoy a meal. At a women's event five years ago, twenty of us went to a very nice Italian restaurant. The seat to my left was vacant, and a woman I did not know sat down next to me. She immediately started to tell us that she was on a diet plan and carbos were history to her.

This woman went on and on, looking for others to join in and validate her. She then proceeded to talk about how much exercise she engages in with the woman across from her. I was intrigued and listened. The two of them discussed pounds they lost, new exercises they were doing, and how many calories a day they ate. It was quite exhausting to hear, and the conversation was heating up.

The waiter brought us baskets of hot, homemade Italian bread. The smell alone was pleasing. I could not wait to dig in with fresh grated cheese and garlic olive oil for the dipping.

The woman next to me told us she was not allowed bread, and she moved the basket away after I helped myself to two small pieces. I could feel the anxiety of her body language, as she never stopped talking about calories and carbohydrates. In twenty minutes or so, between sitting down and ordering her meal, she talked herself into that mindset that tomorrow is "Monday," and she should just let loose on that bread basket. Before I knew what had happened, the entire basket of bread was gone, and more was on its way.

Feeling deprived of what you enjoy and focusing on it increases the desire for it to an overwhelming degree. We should enjoy eating, and the taste of some foods is euphoric, but that does not mean we should eat or not eat to abuse ourselves. When you have impulses to give in without taking a step back, you lose the battle. That is why we eat compulsively. We tell ourselves this is the last time, tomorrow is a new day, and we can begin again. Unfortunately for most of us, the self-hatred for failing yet again turns us against ourselves, and when tomorrow comes we don't make it right. We never get close to being healed because our inner critic is still alive and well.

I was this woman and could be her again. What prevents that? I make a choice that I am not going to listen to the inner critic and let food control me. I will allow myself a little pleasure. Once I make peace with food in this way, my soul and body fall in line with the bigger plan. I allow myself to have the bread, and the interest subsides. I do not obsess about it. I can wait until the next time. I do not have to have everything right then and there. If I do, it is because *I allow it.*

If you are struggling and fighting with food and this inner critic, there is a healthier way to live. It is time to allow yourself to break free of fighting with the so-called forbidden foods. Learn to enjoy them, and who knows, you may decide you do not want them. You may be saying, "No. I can't do it." I am telling you to do it and *trust yourself.* It may take time, but doing this tells the inner critic, "Shut up! I am in control and am a wonderful human being, worthy of enjoying food at a meal with friends."

The outcome is a home run, breaking free of the craziness in our heads that takes away joy. You might and probably will feel guilty until you establish new ways of thinking, but hang in there! It works. It is crucial to understand that you have choices. To think and believe that you are in control is the cornerstone that will enable you to succeed in *getting healthy though your weight loss journey.*

Believing the inner critic is holding on to a fantasy, the lie that you are bad because you enjoy all kinds of food, the lie that you are only good when you eat the "good" foods. Shut it down. Stop the insanity in your head. You can do it! *You are stronger than you think.* Stop beating yourself up for every morsel you were told was poison for you. It is time to *stop dieting.* You know that diets do not work over time, so stop thinking in those terms. Look at food as *fuel* for your body and learn how to enjoy eating.

The inner critic is a liar. You have the right to eat whatever you want, when you want it, and to eat how much you want. The problem is that some of us do not know when to stop. The inner critic also makes us feel the need to eat it all at one time. This *all or nothing* attitude is also a lie. We can eat anything we want at any time. Knowing this truth, I will not eat it all and promise myself I will eat healthy tomorrow. No! I will eat what I want today. I will enjoy it. And I have the security of knowing I can eat again tomorrow. This way of thinking gives me the freedom to let go of the food, to even decide I don't want it now, because I can also have it tomorrow.

It is a great and liberating feeling to eat what you want guilt-free. You shut down the inner critic and stop the destructive cycle of guilt and self-hatred, which leads to more binging, which confirms how bad and worthless you are, and so on. Crushing this voice is the first step toward an entirely different life in which *you*, not food, control your life. As a health professional who has worked with women for over twenty years, I have heard women tell of this voice that controls their moods. When they silence it and re-program their thinking, they begin to experience freedom from guilt and shame — the freedom to enjoy and control food.

There is not a women or man who does not want instant gratification when dealing with weight loss. This is the false promise of the diet and fitness industries. Those who lose weight and exercise focus on their physical body alone, and they eventually struggle to keep the weight off and stay in shape because their thinking has not been challenged and changed. Once the weight is off, I ask them, "What happens next? Now what?" Most do not think beyond reaching their body shape goal.

The inner critic is still alive and well, telling them how good they are for achieving their goal, but reminding them that they have never been able to maintain it. Eventually, the evil voice drives their impulses, and they begin to go back to their old behavior, eating the way they used to eat. Little by little, the weight comes back. So, the inner critic has run the whole show: shame, diet and exercise, feeling good instead of bad, doubting yourself, giving in to old habits — and it all confirms what a worthless, terrible person you are.

The first step to stop this cycle of self-destruction is to crush the inner critic by making the decision not to listen, trusting yourself, allowing yourself to enjoy food, and learning to exercise your will power to control food. Stop believing the lie that "you can't help yourself" and stand firmly in the truth that you are in charge and *can* help yourself!

> *So above all, guard the affections of your heart,*
> *for they affect all that you are. Pay attention*
> *to the welfare of your innermost being, for*
> *from there flows the wellspring of life.*
>                                   *Proverbs 4:23* TPT

# 7

## California Dreaming —
## Living in Fear and Chaos

*A*fter I graduated high school, I was restless. While others were planning for college or marriage, I had a stirring in my soul to travel the globe. I thought I would be happier living somewhere else. If I were in a relationship, he would love me. Maybe, if I had different friends, my life would be better. Not having a life plan or goals, I worked for a big publishing company during the day and was a part-time server at a popular dinner theatre on the main line at night.

The day job was boring, but my serving job was exciting. I got to meet other free spirits like me. The money was great, and I loved the job. While there, I met two women who also had big dreams that did not involve staying in Philly. Neither Franny nor Judy wanted to live at home, go to college, or get married. We all wanted to travel, to be footloose and fancy free. After all, it was the 1970's!

After weeks of talking about taking off, the three of us decided to move to the Bay area in California and become hippies. The plan was to use my car, hitch a trailer containing minimal belongings, and take off for the West Coast. We still needed to save some money, but within months we were ready. We decided to take some time to see some of the country on the way.

Prior to leaving, we all met at Judy's apartment, hopped on her bed, and rolled a joint. We opened a huge map, blindfolded ourselves, and each of us pinned a place to visit on the road to San Francisco. Yep, that is how we would do it. When we opened our eyes, we had pinned Kalamazoo, Michigan; Waco, Texas; and Denver, Colorado. So that was the route we would take with trailer in tow. We would take turns driving, and soon we would be off.

When I told my mother what my plans were, she was not happy; but she knew she could not hold me back. It had been two years since I graduated from high school, and I was ready to make my own choices. She never believed I would make it on my own and told me I would be back. I was scared but determined to make it.

The three amigos took off for Kalamazoo, Michigan, our first stop on the map. I am not sure how long we stayed, but it was cold and rainy for the entire time we were there. We stayed with a couple of guys, who had a farm house. They were friends of Judy's. We then took off for Texas and somehow landed in Santé Fe, New Mexico, a place of color and Zen. We hung out there for a couple of days and really got to see the town, with its wonderful culture and lots of art studios. This was my first experience exploring new foods and cultures, as I grew up in an Italian, Catholic neighborhood. The trip opened my eyes to how differently some people lived, and it was a new world.

On our last morning in Santa Fe, I had to fill up the car, so we stopped at a gas station on the outskirts of town.

As I began to pump the gas, out of nowhere four police cars surrounded my car. The officers emerged with guns loaded and ready to shoot. All I remember seeing were gun barrels staring at me. Franny, Judy, and I were taken in for questioning. We thought they knew we had pot and cocaine in the glove compartment of my car, and that was why they were busting us. Far from it!

There had been a bank robbery in town, and the getaway car matched my car's description, with a redhead in the driver seat (I had red hair). I told them it was not me, but I was told to be quiet. I was so scared, but after a line-up and finger printing we were released. They could not apologize enough. The bank teller had identified the actual driver. We were told not to leave town for a few hours, but when we checked in with the police later that day, they said we were free to go. We were on our way to San Francisco to live our new lives.

We stopped in Los Angeles before heading up the Coast, and we stayed with another server from Philly named Helene, who had left for LA before we did. She lived in Topanga Canyon with her boyfriend, a music producer from Scotland. We drove up the Canyon, and when we got to the top, the view was unbelievable. At that time, all the up-and-coming bands lived in the Canyon. I got to hang out with the Eagles and Super Tramp. I met Glen Frye, whom I adored. He was the nicest guy.

About a week later, we arrived in San Francisco and temporarily stayed with Franny's aunt and uncle. They both had drinking problems and were probably alcoholics, so our welcome wore out quickly. Living with the nonstop fighting and seeing them passed out every night was not worth having a roof over our heads.

Judy got a place in Noe Valley, Franny stayed with her aunt and uncle, and I wandered around homeless. I had my car, which was my sanctuary. All I heard in my head was my mother telling me I would never make it. I was determined to survive, and I did.

I have some wonderful and vivid memories of my life in San Francisco. It was enchanted, magical, and so laid-back. This was a monumental time for me, my first time away from home alone. Still, I spent the first Christmas alone and so lonely. I was hanging out at a local park, met some people, and they invited me home with them for dinner. I shared a meal with some locals, who adopted me. There were other people there who were invited, and I would hang out with them weekly. I was so naïve in those days, but I still had the sense to take care of myself.

Going to the Castro area was captivating. I met drag queens, homosexuals, and transsexuals and felt like a kid in a candy store, looking for my next fix. Castro was a world unto itself, partying day and night. This was a place where you could be whatever and whoever you wanted, and no one judged you. You could hide within yourself, away from the outside world.

I meandered to the Height/Ashbury part of town and met many drifters like myself. The bars were packed all day long, and you could buy cocaine and heroin anytime or anywhere. It was so free. People were just so easy-going, and life was different. We were all free birds, with not a concern in life. Hanging in coffee shops in San Francisco, you could meet the locals and possibly find a roommate. Noe Valley was the happening place to live in the 1970's, and I wanted to live there. With so many drifters in town looking for roommates, I was sure to find one, and I did.

I found an ad on the Noe Valley marketplace bulletin board. A guy named Michael was looking for a roommate. I called him, we met, and we hit it off. He was a teacher from Chicago who had transferred to the Bay area. He needed a change of scenery like I did, so he secured a teaching job at a San Francisco high school. From that day on, we hung out together a lot. I think he moved to San Francisco questioning his sexuality. He told me that gay men were always hitting on him, and he asked me one night if I thought he could be gay. I was not sure, but I questioned why any straight man would hang out in the Castro area.

Together we found a great three-bedroom apartment on 21st and Delores Street. I was right across the street from Judy. Franny had gone back home, and I never heard from her again. Michael and I eventually found a third roommate, Danny, who was a kind and sweet musician. He spent most nights at his girlfriend's, so Michael and I did not see him much. I thought that I had finally found my peace and paradise. Life was great, or so I thought.

I eventually got a waitress job at Sutter Street Station, at the end of the trolley car line in downtown San Francisco. I worked the day shift, and the crowd was mostly blue-collar construction workers, who were working at the Pacific Building across the street. The money was good, and I had regulars who came in to see me. I never met the owner, but eventually I learned that Margo, my manager, was a madam. One of Margo's bartenders was a big, busty, platinum blonde with long, fake fingernails, false eyelashes, and an annoying laugh. The men loved her.

When I worked the night shift, Margo told me to be very nice to the executives. I told her I was. "No," she said very nicely. What did she mean? I found out when one of Margo's boy toys, Tom the night drunk, watched the bar while she took someone in the bathroom for his sexual pleasure. I also would see her hugging and grabbing men inappropriately. She would ask me to pour drinks while she "made the rounds." I was so naïve, my mouth dropped open the first time I witnessed her in action. I stayed because I needed the money, but that place was the devils' den.

Judy introduced me to the Noe Valley bar called Finnegan's Wake. I quickly became a regular there, since I lived in the neighborhood. Finnegan's Wake was a hippie, red-neck hangout, and the locals packed it day and night. That was where I met Mark, the love of my life. He and I were two lonely souls drawn together by my need for love and his need for the next fix. He was alone, I was alone, and so we hooked up. I immediately fell in love with him.

Mark and I were hippies, who lived in overalls and Birkenstocks. It was the era of sex, drugs, and rock 'n roll. The night I met him, I can remember hearing angels singing. He was adorable, sweet, and a southern charmer. It was much later in our relationship that I would acknowledge his dark side. I outweighed him by at least fifty pounds, but he was not bothered by that. He was a musician and had his sights set on becoming the next Neal Young. He played the guitar with such passion, but drugs and alcohol were his first love.

I loved Mark despite his addiction. I would change him. I would help him get clean and sober. I worked, and he was stoned every day. He was sleeping on his brother's couch, but soon he was staying with me a lot. His brother warned me that he was bad news, but I was going change him.

One night, high on cocaine and alcohol, he came to my apartment on a rampage. I looked at him and saw a demon in his face. He was strung out on some bad drugs. If Michael hadn't been there, Mark might have killed me. Michael found him trying to strangle me while banging my head against the wall. The cops came, they threw Mark in jail, and the next day he remembered nothing. I loved him and took him back. When sober, he was the sweetest, gentlest soul; but when he was using, he would freak out and I would be devastated. My heart broke with sadness, as I knew it was just a matter of time until this relationship exploded.

I was twenty when I found out I was pregnant. I was sick every day. Mark could not find a job, he had no money, and his brother wanted him out. We were getting high together, and I was now living on welfare. Kids were not in the plan. I still had hopes for a future with Mark and was so in love. I wanted this to work, as I saw the compassionate and caring person he could be.

Two days after telling him I was pregnant, Mark was nowhere to be found. His mother had sent him a ticket to Florida to live with his parents. I have often wondered about him, but I never saw him again. I decided to abort the baby and reacted to the abortion like I reacted to everything else: I ate, did drugs, and hung out with toxic people. I didn't tell anyone what had happened. I kept my life so chaotic, that I had no time to grieve.

After this disastrous relationship, two earthquakes, a housing problem, and missing my family, I returned to Philly. I didn't care what my mother had said.

# 8

# Rocky Mountain High — My First Fitness Class

*I came into this world queen-size. I was ten pounds when I was born. I knew somebody had to be a queen in this world — why not me? I was the third in line out of six kids. I had an older brother and sister, younger sister, and two younger brothers. We were a very close family with great parents. Even as the fat girl with low self-esteem, I always knew I was loved. We were a loving family but dysfunctional. I was shy. I was fat. I was the girl who couldn't run in gym class or run around. I always watched the babies because I really didn't go out to play.*

*Mom had so many kids and was out working. At forty-two, my dad got sick and couldn't work. He had a bad heart. He had worked three jobs at one time to support six kids. My sister was involved in so many activities. I took care of all the kids. I was Daddy's girl. My mother worked, and there were so many kids. I cleaned and looked after the little ones. I never doubted I was loved. I knew early I was an outcast as a fat girl. When the other kids were playing, I'd sit and read something. Or take care of other people.*

*I was always afraid of men and didn't date. My older sister was beautiful. My younger sister was sporty and cute. I just wanted to blend in. I didn't go out and didn't think I deserved to be loved. It wasn't until I met my future husband that I got involved with someone. I met him in church. I just knew he was the one. He made me feel loved at the beginning. We met at the Harvest Ball, a church social.*

*I'm cleaning up after the party. I dropped some stuff off a tray. I said to myself, "If this is meant to be, he'll pick up my stuff." And he did. I had a date to go bowling with someone else from the church. I didn't make it, because I went out with Joe. I was about a size eighteen back then. That night we went to a hotel. A nice Catholic girl. But love was something I wanted to experience. I was head over heels. Within three months I knew we would get married. Head over heels, madly deeply, truly in love, I thought.*

*He was a Eucharistic minister in the church, as I was. We planned a fairytale life together and a wedding. If someone deserved a fairytale wedding, it was Sally. Joe had a bus company. I thought he had money. He drove a Towne Car. It was like Donna Reed. This is how it was meant to be. Sally and Joe looked so happy together, so people were happy for us. I don't know if I was ever really in love, but I did love the way I felt with him back then.*

*Joe came from a dysfunctional family — alcoholism. Sally had to take care of him. The mother hen. Here was this guy who I thought loved me for who I am. I did what society told me I should have done. I played the part; let me make him my all and all. I was ashamed that I made him my everything and not my God. I've always had a spiritual side to me, even as a child. I walked away from it. I wanted to be a nun at one time. I think I hid behind him. I think society influenced me to let him run the show.*

*We got married. Nice big wedding. I knew he had a past that he wasn't so proud of, but Sally was going to heal that. It was a beautiful wedding. The first thing he does on our wedding night, he counted the money. Here I am all dolled up. But nothing. We lived with his grandmother, and I always felt uncomfortable there. We did save up and got our own home. It was nice.*

*I was very much sheltered as a child. I missed my family. That feeling of the fat little girl, the outsider never left me. That's why I ate the cookies and candy and the chips. It's 8 o'clock — snack time! I never felt I belonged in that home with him. Because the emotion in the relationship changed. Three months into my marriage it was over. Coming home from shopping, I remember dropping a roll of paper towels as I was going up the steps, and my husband got angry and threw the paper towels. What I didn't realize then was he was trying to hit me with them. Then he threw me down the steps.*

*At the time, I told myself I fell; but I know now he tripped me. Four months into the marriage he raped me. He…took me with so much violence…. There was no way he was touching me after that. No way. And I ate everything under the sun and moon, so no one would find me attractive. When I was a child I liked to eat, but this was different. I began to hide behind the fat suit. I added a whole other layer of padding to myself, so he couldn't get to me. I hid behind it. It was my comfort zone*

*I could still see feel the pain of what he did to me. He broke my leg in the process of raping me. It still hurts today. Afterward, I felt lower than low — a second-class citizen. And I questioned my faith. Where was my God while this was going on? "Lord —*

*you said you loved me and I gave you my
all. You are not there for me. So, this man
said he loves me, but he hurts me. Maybe
this is how it's supposed to be for me. Maybe
it's not supposed to ever be any better.*

—*Sally*

Right after high school, I visited my aunt and uncle, who
lived in the Denver area. I fell in love with the mountains and wanted to live there someday. Following my difficult time in San Francisco and after spending some time in
Philly with my family, I decided to move to Denver. I would
live with my aunt and uncle until I got a job and could afford
my own place.

I met Bob at the Jester Lounge. His roommate introduced us, and we really hit it off. It wasn't long before we
were living together. Sometimes, he and I would go out
for breakfast, and I would have a double order of creamed
chipped beef on toast, a bagel and cream cheese, and fried
potatoes. I gained more and more weight, but I couldn't see
it. I was in total denial about it, and Bob didn't care. He
loved me as I was.

I felt differently. After eating, I had terrible remorse.
Most times, I wanted to throw up from disgust. The inner
critic would let me have it with, "You're a pig. You're horrible. Why did you do this?" Physically, I couldn't breathe.
Emotionally, I was drowning. I was eating out of such distress that I didn't fully taste anything. I would snack during
the day, and we'd have a big dinner when he got home and ice
cream after that. I was blind to see what harm I was causing
myself. Bob would sit and drink his beer, and I would eat
and feel sick. It was the same ritual every day. I hated myself.

I thought if I addressed my weight problem, everything else would be healed. If I lost some weight and got myself physically fit, the emotional issues would be better. I would look at myself in the mirror every day (although, I became very good at looking at myself from the neck up), and everywhere I looked there was all this fat hanging off my body. It was a reminder of how crazy I was, how toxic my relationships were, how my mother let me down, and how my childhood was full of trauma.

I felt like being fat was a way of writing everything in my head across my body. It reflected the chaos in my mind. My mind was on overload all the time, and I knew I was destined to have a dreadful life if I didn't do something. Every day, I would swear to myself, "Today is the day. I will go on a diet, eat less, start to move, and make the changes to insure my thinness." Sad to say, my Monday never came. My world continued to consist of my food addiction and Bob's alcoholism. It was a perfect co-dependent relationship, just two addicts feeding off each other. He let me eat, and I let him drink. We gave each other permission to destroy ourselves.

We moved to Cheyenne, Wyoming, to be near Bob's family, and I hit bottom with my food addiction. I can vividly remember that morning. Bob had left for work, and I was settling down to my normal breakfast ritual: a half rack of ribs, four eggs dripping in butter, a package of Pillsbury biscuits, and two large glasses of orange juice. Sitting on the couch in my favorite mumu gown, watching a game show or soap opera, I felt a sharp pain shoot across my chest. I had never experienced anything like it. It felt like somebody was stabbing me. I thought I was having a heart attack and my life was ending. No! I was too young! I had my life ahead of me! How did I get to this place? How did I let myself become this big? How could I change it? What did I need to do?

These thoughts went through my mind as I headed to the ER with our neighbor, Jerry. They did tests but couldn't find anything wrong. The doctor told me it could be any number of issues, and I should follow up with my family doctor. I did not have a family doctor. Because of my weight, I was too embarrassed to visit a doctor; but this scared me enough to consider an appointment.

I found a local doctor through my neighbor. I was petrified over what I would be told. My weight was the issue. It was always the issue. When I arrived at the office, it was very dismal and quiet. The walls were an ugly, chalky color, and there weren't even any magazines. There were no paintings on the walls or music to hum to, and the receptionist was not very friendly. I wanted to cancel and go home, but then I remembered that chest pain and stayed.

Wow, I was in for a rude awakening. The doctor was very straightforward. He looked me in the eyes and said, "You need to lose weight. How did you become this big?" I could not speak. With head down, face red from embarrassment, my eyes welling up, and my heart sinking, I felt humiliated. Someone was finally declaring what the inner critic had told me all along: I was bad because of my weight. I felt like a criminal being sentenced for a crime.

How could he say those things to me? My love (Bob, the food enabler) wanted me bigger, and the world was telling me to get smaller. Who should I listen to? It was hard for me to face what I had been denying for years: I was fat and unhealthy. I was overwhelmed and scared for my future. Hearing those words, "You need to lose weight," pierced every sore spot. No overweight person wants to hear it. Those words are like a dagger in the heart.

I felt numb, like I had been punched in the face. I had lost weight before, but no one loved me. As a young girl, my grandmother repeatedly told me to be thin to get a man. Well, I was not thin, but I had a man. I felt loved now. I knew I was fat, but did others realize how big I was? Did they matter? I was living with someone who thought I was fine just as I was. He loved me. He loved my body. He loved how I took care of him and let him drink. He loved that I would never leave.

All this streamed through my head in my most vulnerable emotional state. I couldn't understand that the doctor was genuinely trying to help me. I heard his words as criticism and condemnation. In my mind, he was calling me unlovable and worthless. I walked out of his office, had a pity party, and cried until my eyes hurt. That did not change the fact that I knew what needed to be done.

I was fat, unhealthy, and needed to do whatever it took. I would have to challenge every part of who I was. I took a deep breath and said to myself, "You need to get real and own up to the fact that *you* are killing yourself. You are grossly obese, unhealthy, and in a toxic relationship with someone who does not love you. You are living life based on lies and fantasy. *You* have to get yourself together or *you* are going to die."

That was my "ah-ha" moment. This was my time. I hated Cheyenne and convinced Bob that we needed to go back to Denver. There, my life would start on a path to wellness. Going to that doctor and hearing those words changed something on the inside of me. But, *Where do I begin?*

I told myself, "Take a deep breath, have the conversation, and tell yourself that you can do this, you need to do this, your life depends on this, and you will take one step at a time one day at a time." Every diet I had ever been a victim to needed to be erased from my mind. I had to make dieting a thing of the past. It was not going to be easy, but I was on a *new me journey*, and what a ride I was in for!

I started going to the library and reading everything I could find on nutrition. The articles were limited, but I was determined that nothing and nobody would stop me. I needed to figure this out on my own, and I was determined that it was time to focus on me and what I needed. I needed this to be all about *me*. I became driven to thrive not just survive.

I was glad to be back in Denver, where I drove by a gym every day and would watch skinny people going in and coming out. Every time, I would ask myself, "What do they do in there?" I figured they must know the secret to staying thin. I wanted to know it too. Day after day, I would sit in my car, watching and thinking about going in the door; however, I was petrified of the ridicule I might encounter. What would they say about my body? Could they make me feel any lower than I already felt?

I would say to myself, "Get out of the car and just go up there," and panic would set in. The inner critic would shut me down with, "You are fat. They will stare at you. Everyone will be laughing. *You* do not deserve to look or feel better." Then I would drive home. I went through this for about a month, and finally I had had enough. It was time to make my move. I took a deep breath, and something clicked in my head. I knew God was with me, and I heard a gentle, loving voice say, "Just do it and stop thinking about it." After feeling so emotionally battered and beaten down, I was now in survivor mode. This motivated me to take that leap of faith and go where I had never gone before.

I opened the front door of the health club, looked up, and saw the "stairway to heaven." The front door was at the top of a long set of steps. This almost prompted me to leave. I had to tell myself, "You are not defeated. You are not pitiful. You are powerful." I ascended, one step at a time. At the halfway mark, I had to sit down because I was panting and sweating profusely. I thought I was having a heart attack. I sat on those steps and cried. It was so painful. The inner critic began to creep up, and I began to hear words of defeat. I had always felt useless and unworthy, but this was worse than ever.

I returned home, sobbing and questioning everything about myself. "What is my life about? What is my purpose? Why am I in this relationship with this man?" As I questioned myself, a sense of calm come over me. Something inside me said, "It's going to be okay. All this weight on your shoulders is going to diminish. You will see. The best is yet to come!"

It took a few days to get myself motivated again. I went back and was determined to get up those steps. I had a plan, and I was going to get up those steps if it took me all day. I opened the door, looked up, and said to myself, "Get up those steps and do not look back." As I began to walk up one step at a time, I could feel myself almost there. I could see the journey. I could see the finish. I got to the top and opened the door. I did it!

As I opened the door, I met John. He was the man who would put me on the path to better health. John was a bodybuilder, who had enormous veins and muscles on every inch of his body. I can still remember his smile, compassion, and warmth towards this young, plus size-woman, who feared life itself. He said, "Can I help you? Are you here to work out?"

I froze and did not know what to say. Workout? Me? What does that even mean? My brain was on overload. I had just walked up a flight of steps that had taken my breath away! *I'm probably too fat to work out, right? Can a 300-pound-plus woman do aerobics?* I must have shaken my head yes, as I heard him say, "Well, you've come to the right place. There's an aerobics class starting in a couple of minutes. Do you want to take it?" John never looked at my body, but he knew I needed help. God sent me an angel with big, bulging muscles.

Before I knew it, I was taking my very first fitness class. This was the beginning of the dawn of the fitness era. There wasn't a woman in that class who weighed more than 110 pounds. The attire that the ladies wore was shiny leotards, leg warmers, and sweat bands, the kind that Olivia Newton John worn in the "Let's Get Physical" video. I, on the other hand, wore baggy, fleece-lined, men's sweat pants with holes between the legs where my thighs rubbed together, a big man's sweatshirt, and old sneakers. I was sweating just standing there, but I told myself, *You are here. This is what you came for. Now, just do it.*

I stood in the back of the room, so no one could see or hear me. I had no idea what I was in for. Then Kathy, our aerobics instructor, appeared. She was tall and slender, and the epitome of a beautiful woman to me. She was also incredibly sweet and never made me feel uncomfortable. She said, "Take a place and let's get moving!"

They were all so welcoming to me. When I opened that door and walked through it, my life changed forever. There surely is a Heaven, and I was getting a little glimpse of it here. The women in that room could have made fun of me or made me feel ridiculous. That happens every day to larger women who go into health clubs. I am so grateful for that first five minutes, when John had the goodness to treat me with sensitivity. If I'd been mocked, made fun of, or turned away, I probably would have gone home and gained another hundred pounds. That one small act of kindness became my miracle and started me into the recovery and freedom I am still experiencing today.

I was so embarrassed in that class, but when I looked around to see who was watching me, it appeared nobody was paying attention. They were all "in the zone," working to follow Kathy's instructions. At first, I could only hear the inner critic saying, "What are you doing here? You're a fat pig. You're with that alcoholic. Both losers." However, the support and kindness of these people drowned it out, and I kept moving and breathing for dear life. My inner dialogue was now saying "Keep going. Keep going. Don't stop. You can do this. You must do this. You've failed at everything else in your life. Don't let them see you quit." I wanted to, but I never quit.

At the end of the first half of the class, Kathy said it was time to do floor work. *Floor work? What is that? Wait, you want me to lie down? Do you see my size? When you're 300-plus pounds, you don't just get on the floor.* Well, I lowered myself hanging onto one of the machines that surrounded us and got down onto the floor. Lying in a supine position, looking at the ceiling, I thought, *How will I get up? Who will be there for me? No, this is not happening. Kathy, do you see how big I am? Are you kidding?*

I was so hot, tired, and sweaty by then, I was panting. Every cell in my body was turning red, but I was not about to give up. I did the floor work. I huffed and puffed my way through it. I finished — or something close to it. Cathy said, "Okay, great class!" I was still on the floor and literally could not move. How was I going to get up? I was screaming inside, and then my angel with bulging muscles appeared with a few other body builders. They came out of the weight room to haul me up from the floor. They were so strong, they lifted me up vertically!

They kept telling me how inspiring I was. *Me? Inspiring? Are you kidding? Really?* They treated me with respect and dignity. It was a turning point I will never forget. A literal gift from God. I drove home, showered, and went right to bed. The next morning, I awoke to a kind of pain I'd never experienced. I felt like I'd been hit by a truck. I told Bob, "I can't move."

Bob went to work, and I stayed in bed and cried, but the tears were two-fold: I was in physical pain, and this kind of pain was new and scary. My life was in turmoil, and I was going to have to change some basic things about how I lived. It was frightening to be dependent on a relationship with food and a toxic, dysfunctional partner and consider that both might be taken away if I continued on this journey. I say, "taken away," because it felt like an outside force was stripping me of my security blanket. It's easier to stay with the status quo than to let go of destructive behavior and people and recover, but I knew I was heading into complete disaster if I stayed. I had to let go of the food and the abusive relationship.

About four days later, I was starting to feel less sore. The phone rang, and it was John from the gym. "We haven't seen you."

I was surprised and made up an excuse. "Oh, well, I wasn't sure about the membership."

He said, "Just come in, and we'll talk about it."

I had not told Bob, because any notion of my getting better, smaller, or healthier only brought out the rage in him that I might eventually leave him. So, I went back to the gym and started going three or four times a week when he wasn't home. I used the machines and took classes. I followed Kathy's routine and learned the moves. She did the same class and wore the same thing every day. I wore the same baggy clothes, so Bob could not tell I was losing weight. He was so wrapped up in his addiction, it was a while before he noticed.

I knew that when he figured out what I was doing, he would be threatened. I started formulating a plan to leave, even though I had no close girlfriends or family near me. It was just me, my two dogs, and Bob. He was rarely sober, and when he was, he shook from the DT's. It took a long time, but he did finally realize what was going on and was very suspicious. He would park his truck outside the health club and wait for me to come out. Then he would scream at me and demand to know what I was up to. He threatened to kill me many times, and there was no doubt in my mind that he was capable of it. By that time, however, I was motivated and inspired to take control of my life.

The plan was to leave Bob, and I knew I had to go underground when I finally left him. Barbara and Danny, my neighbors, would come over to my house and try to get me to leave. One was in recovery and the other came from an alcoholic family. Neither of them drank, but they knew I was a caretaker. Together, they helped me plan to hide, taking my two dogs. I was no longer going to allow Bob to push me around. I was petrified, but I was on a mission to save my life.

In the past, when I had tried to make positive changes, I always started by going on a diet. I had tried so many diets and failed at all of them. Each time, I ended up fatter than before I began. This time, I began by moving my body, and soon it was clear that something was changing. I felt differently. I felt stronger, braver, and more energetic. I started having a sense of pride that I had never experienced before. I began to feel invested in myself. Fitness would become my saving grace.

One day Kathy had a car issue and could not teach her class. Somebody said, "Hey, Deb, you know the routine. Why don't you teach the class?"

I laughed, "Yeah, sure." But they were serious! John asked me if I thought I could do it. Before thinking about it I said, "Yes, I'll give it a try." Little did I realize what I said yes to. The most frightening scenario was suddenly staring me in the face: twenty people needed my direction. No mirrors. Just blank faces waiting for me to get them moving.

Initially, I went blank. Then I managed to begin with the first move and get through the class with lots of motivation. I told them I was screaming to myself, "Never give up!" After that, John put me on the schedule to teach some classes, and that began my love affair with teaching fitness to others while moving my own body. This was one of the first memories from that time of my life that was good. I had a hard time shaking too many bad memories, but this was one I never wanted to shake!

# 9

# Healing with Exercise

There are many benefits of exercise, and they are highly touted. Moving your body is great for the heart and lungs. Exercise will lower your blood pressure and bad cholesterol, strengthen your bones, help you sleep, increase metabolism, and burn fat. Many of the mind/body fitness routines can help retrain our brains. Over the past twenty years, studies have shown how physical activity can strengthen the structure, function, and chemistry of our brains. This change in the biology of our brain affects how we think and reason, our sensory experiences, and our emotional behavior.

Exercise leaves an imprint on the brain that has been shown to prevent several psychiatric problems, including depression and anxiety. The brain is not permanently hardwired; it is continuously changing. When we exercise, it reacts in a similar way to the way the body reacts: by getting stronger. It develops new neurons, new pathways between neurons, and more blood vessels. After cardio exercise, the brain also secretes endorphins, the chemicals that make you feel fantastic. Endorphins increase your sense of well-being, boost your energy, and elevate your mood. That feeling has been referred to as a "runner's high," and it can help create self-esteem and a more optimistic outlook on life.

## Mental Barriers to Exercise

Feeling self-consciousness is very understandable when you are in unknown territory. Nobody wants to feel embarrassed in front of people, especially in a fitness center. It was not my life's goal to feel like the "fat girl on the treadmill." And some of us don't feel like we are worthy of working out. When we already blame ourselves for failing to control our eating, who needs to add another failure to the list?

Many have the notion that we diet to lose weight. Some think we must lose weight before we can think about exercise. We have been culturally conditioned to believe that fitness is only for the fit. For the overweight woman, the idea of moving her body can be scary, especially in public. Fitness centers are not typically comfortable environments for larger women. Those who have experienced abuse have even more sensitivity about their bodies. The notion of working out and having people stare at our bodies can be highly intimidating.

The Center for Obesity Research and Education at Temple University studied hundreds of obese women, who joined a program encouraging them to be active. They reported several things that hindered them from exercising:

1. Feeling self-conscious
2. Not wanting to fail
3. Fearing injury
4. Perceived poor health
5. Having minor aches and pains
6. Feeling too overweight to exercise

Will you make it through a cardio class? Will you be able to do the moves? Can you stick with it? Concerns about your physical ability to exercise are normal and should be addressed. You say to yourself, "Am I really healthy enough for this? Shouldn't I lose weight first? Gee, I already have so many aches and pains. I can't imagine being more physically uncomfortable." You don't want to get hurt or feel more pain, physically and emotionally.

I thought and felt all those things for a very long time. I didn't know you don't have to begin a fitness program in public if you don't want to. Choose a fitness DVD that is friendly to plus-size women, like the *ShapelyGirl* fitness™ series, and do it in the privacy in your living room. Buy a treadmill or bike for your home. How about a walking buddy? But if you choose to join a fitness center, take a deep breath and have a positive conversation with yourself. Most people don't care about what you are doing or are even paying attention to you. In fact, they might admire you for having the courage to get started.

Most likely, the feeling of inferiority is coming from you. Start moving for *you*. Exercise and moving my body saved my life. It allowed me the freedom to take charge of what I needed the most: to feel good about who I was. To you, I say, "Take a deep breath and begin to move and feel better. Dance around, laugh, and take charge of your life. Do it now!" Let people think what they want to think. *You* take care of *you*. I did it and so can you.

## Getting Off the Couch *Now*

I was always waiting to get a life once I lost weight, and I waited for years. It took me a long time to finally come to terms with the truth: I had no idea what an ideal weight was.

You can't wait until you are the ideal weight to start loving yourself. There is a place for you in the world of fitness, and it is essential that you find that place as part of your recovery. The longer you wait to be skinny, the more time you are wasting. Now is the time to get up and move!

Stop obsessing about dieting and waiting for your body to shrink with some crazy, magical, fad diet. We both know this kind of diet will never get you there. But if you get up and start walking or taking a class, then you can begin to get fit. An important thing to keep in mind when starting is not only to keep going but also have compassion towards yourself. So many times, we start programs, and if we do not finish, we think we are unsuccessful. You need to go at *your* pace, not anyone else's. The fact that you are moving is success.

Taking the first step is tough; it was the hardest decision for me, for sure. I decided to change my life, and this took many years not two months. You must practice patience instead of unrealistic expectations. After all, trying diet after diet and failing for so long, it stands to reason that you will be expecting to fail once again and give up. The results you will start to notice from an exercise program will be accrued over a long period of time. You can't jump in and out when you feel like it; you must stay committed and accountable to yourself and to someone else. Sticking with your fitness goals will help you feel the benefits and make changes you can live with over a lifetime.

People ask me this question all the time: "How long did it take you to lose your weight?" My answer is the same today as it was ten years ago" I took one day at a time, one meal at a time, and today I am still working on it. My goal was always to feel better, look better, and heal from the trauma in my past.

Right now, make this commitment to yourself: "I will incorporate movement into my life, and when challenges and setbacks come my way, I will tell myself that this is part of life and it will pass shortly. If I feel like I am slipping, I'll take a day off and get a massage. I'll breathe deep and get back in the game immediately. But I will never give up! That is not an option."

## Making Peace with Your Body

*Eleven years ago, I weighed 270 pounds and was squeezing into a size 24. In 1998, I joined a local women's gym. I started out walking on a treadmill but found it very boring, so I decided to try a class: Debra Mazda's ShapelyGirl Workout. Right away, I related to Debra's personal story, as she explained her own struggles and triumphs with weight and exercise. She was energetic, funny, and encouraging. I couldn't believe that this woman who was so strong and fit once weighed as much as I did! That gave me so much hope. And I loved the fact that other larger women were in the class with me, and we were all in the battle together. During "circle time" discussions after the workout we were able to offer each other support.*

*After several months of doing Debra's workout twice a week, I lost about 50 pounds. I felt so excited and motivated to do even more to challenge myself. I used*

*Debra's ShapelyGirl Let's Get Moving DVD and took off another 35. Debra Mazda has been my inspiration through all of the ups and downs. Even when I found myself facing a very stressful time and began slipping into my old bad habits, I was able to enlist Debra's help to get me back on track. Debra's strategies for controlling emotional eating, smart nutrition and learning to enjoy exercise has made me realize that I can be in control of my body, my weight, and my mind. Probably the most important lesson I learned from Debra is that I can be fit and fabulous at a size 14. When I was 270 pounds, I thought I had to be a size 6 to exercise. Debra Mazda showed me that I could start working out at any size and find a new life in the process.*

*— Denise*

If we know we need to get up and move and breathe, then we must make peace with our bodies. It is so easy to divorce yourself from a body you hate, which has been a source of shame. You tell yourself, "I am not my body. I am good; it's my body that's bad." Recovery from Binge Eating Disorder means you must embrace the idea of reuniting with your body. Appreciate it. Recognize what it needs. Respect those needs.

It sounds strange to even think about the need to reconnect with your body, but that is literally what you need to do. For women of all sizes this can be an issue. Thinner women can hate their cellulite and flabby arms and have negative body image issues too. For larger women who have been "living in their heads," it may be necessary to symbolically make friends with their bodies.

Is it time to have that positive conversation with your body and express emotions you might have been hiding? Here are some suggestions to begin:

- I am sorry for hating you.
- I appreciate everything you do for me.
- I am grateful for your strength.
- Forgive me for not always giving you what you need.
- I am a powerful, positive woman; I do not need to feel afraid.
- I will listen to you more closely.
- I love that you show me how to move.
- Thank you for helping me to heal.
- Thank you for allowing me to become healthier, fit, and free from food addiction.
- I will feel proud of the journey we are on together.
- I will not expect perfection, and when we stumble, we'll get up.

## Fitness Comes in Many Sizes

A headline in *The New York Times* not long ago read: "Better to be Fit and Fat than Skinny and Unfit." The article discussed the mounting research that supports the idea that fitness comes in many sizes. You don't have to be skinny to be fit. Weight alone is not an indicator of poor health. There is mounting evidence that despite the excess pounds they may carry, there are people — some of them even obese — who have normal blood pressure, glucose, and cholesterol levels, and are not at high risk for heart disease. Fitness is an important factor.

Studies from the Cooper Institute in Dallas analyzed fitness levels of 66,000 people while the subjects ran on a treadmill. The results showed that heavier people who kept a steady pace on the treadmill had a lower risk of heart disease than those who were slim and could not keep up. This is not to say that we should ignore obesity, but it underscores the importance that size is no excuse. All of us must get moving!

Believe that there is a place for you in the world of fitness. You can have hips and thighs and a shapely body and still work on being healthy. You don't have to get to your ideal weight before you start moving. Decide your weight will no longer give you license to be a couch potato. Not everyone will be a single-digit dress size. Be the best you can be in the body you are in today.

Research also showed that programs like *ShapelyGirl*™ Fitness, which I developed specifically to help women achieve an exercise comfort zone, can be successful. It's all about getting in the zone and feeling like you can do it. Since I lost my weight by learning to love exercise years ago, I have wanted to help create a haven for larger women in the world of fitness. I am glad to know science is finally taking a close look at this need and am happy to be part of a common-sense solution for women of all sizes, who want to get healthy.

Another thing I have learned over the years is that when women have failed on diet after diet, they can also tend to give up on exercise too quickly. Results from working out will be accrued over a long period of time. You can't jump on a scale to measure the changes. I always say, "If you stick to your fitness goals, you will feel the benefits as you make changes that you can live with over a lifetime. Whatever might be hindering you from moving forward, take a deep breath and tell yourself you can get healthy. You deserve to feel better! You can do this, because not only do I believe in you, but I want you to believe in you. *You* can do this, so get up and get moving!"

# 10

## Get Off the Couch and Start Moving

*W*hat Inspired *ShapelyGirl* Fitness™?
In my twenties, I weighed over three hundred pounds and had failed at every diet. I felt hopeless and sometimes wondered how I was going to drag my significant body around another day. Clearly, dieting was not the answer for me. That is when I made a life-changing decision to exercise, and I have never looked back. It took everything I had inside of me to walk up the steps of that fitness center and face my fears.

Starting and finishing my first aerobics class was the biggest achievement of my life up to that point. After that first class, it took two bronzed, muscular, gorgeous body-builders to lift me up from the gym floor. Now, I laugh about it. They were so gentle and understanding. While I hurt all over afterwards, I had the first glimpse of feeling empowered. That glimpse inspired me to continue moving, cut my food portions, and begin to pay attention to what I was putting into my body.

In that glimpse, I found a passion for exercise, and I am still loving it today. By beginning to move and breathe every day, I began to feel better physically and mentally, which enabled me to make better choices in my life. Today, I am happy, positive, and hopeful about the future — not only for me but for you. *ShapelyGirl* Fitness™ was born because I wanted others to find that same success, to say to them, "You can do this!"

My new sense of self inspired me to communicate what I had learned over the years to the millions of other women who were like me. I wanted to give them hope and a fervent passion to never give up, to move their minds and bodies from breakthrough to breakthrough. It was through moving, sweating, and experiencing the amazing benefits of regular exercise that I was able to change my own life more than twenty-five years ago — and so can you.

I was living in Aurora, Colorado, when Richard Simmons came on the scene as a fitness guru. This short, skinny, Afro-haired guy was running around in his signature striped shorts and glittery tank tops, telling the overweight population that they could lose weight with exercise. He told how he had lost his weight by exercising, and he declared that they could do it too. Hollywood took notice, and soon he was on TV, doing interviews, and in magazine articles, spreading his message of compassion for underdog, overweight people.

Before Richard Simmons came on the scene, fitness was for the already fit or skinny people, but he gave those who were overweight the motivation and inspiration to look and feel better. "Hop on board and get moving!" he said. "You can do this like I did." People took notice, and soon he became a household name. Everyone wanted a piece of him, and so did the owners of Holiday Health Clubs. They wanted to use his name and came up with an ingenious idea to open fitness clubs for the underdogs called Richard Simmons Anatomy Asylums. Richard fell for it, and the deal went through while I was in the throes of exercising at my gym.

I would drive by the same strip mall every day, on my way to work as a server at a Mexican restaurant. After work one day, a billboard caught my attention. It said, "Opening Soon – Richard Simmons Anatomy Asylum." I knew his name and stopped by to join. When I walked through the door, I met a woman named Marianna. She was from Romania and had a personality bigger than anyone I had ever met. She was a tall, buxom, redhead with a heavy accent. She had come to America to live the dream.

Marianna worked holidays and was a top sales executive. She could sell you anything and make you believe what she promised would happen. We hit it off, and she offered me a job as her assistant. I had no experience, goals, or plans, but this woman believed in me and told me so. Before I walked out, I was believing her. But did I believe myself? That was the question. Could I do this job she offered me?

Marianna told me later that when she met me, her intuition kicked in and she was sure of me. She knew I was going to go far with her, and she was right. The next day I quit waitressing and said yes to the job. I had no idea what I was getting into, but I knew this decision came from Heaven. I assisted Marianna in presales before clubs opened for business, the first one being the one in Denver. She taught me how to sell memberships and how to make people see what they could not dream about themselves. She also taught me how to run an Anatomy Asylum with excellence and pride.

I worked day and night to prove myself, and it paid off. Once the first club opened, I became the Training Supervisor and was running the show. While the club had a manager and sales staff, my job was to hire instructors whom I thought really had passion to help others to look and feel better not just lose weight. I wanted to hire those who had that spark, a desire in their souls for something great.

With three rooms going all day long, the place was booming morning to night, especially when Richard Simmons was there. People would line up for hours to get through the door just to meet him. I ran classes especially for overweight people, and I hired those who had a burning desire to help others change their lives. This was the beginning of the new era of larger people coming off the couch and beginning to move, and I was right in the middle of it.

It was big honor to work for the Anatomy Asylums. Soon, the first club was booming, which led to multiple clubs. I was traveling to other states to establish clubs, hire instructors, and train them to teach overweight people how to get fit. After a while, I was running more than one club, and I did it with extra pounds on my body. My belief then and today is that you need to be proud of who you are. I found that people related to me and my story. I trained many instructors and loved the job. My instructors were great and very loyal to me, and I was loyal to them. I enjoyed my years there and was heartbroken when the doors closed.

I will always love teaching classes, motivating and inspiring women of every shape, size, and weight. That said, I totally understand how regular exercise is easier said than done. The key to lasting success is not to let exercise overwhelm you. Find out what you like. Do something you enjoy, because when enjoy the activity, you're more likely to stick with it.

Change your workout routine from time to time, but be sure the change is right for you. Just because it is the newest craze does not mean you need to jump on the wagon. I know so many people who jump immediately into the next new diet or fitness craze only to jump out (or crash out) when their expectations are not met.

Another thing to remember is that work, stress, relationships, and busyness can all stand in the way of a regular exercise routine. That is why most Americans don't exercise enough. It's important to figure out what will work for you right now and make a schedule you can stick with. Then you can make exercise a regular part of your life. It also helps to get into a community of likeminded people, who will lift you up not bring you down.

As a fitness professional, I know everyone needs to get off their couch and get moving, but each of us does it for different reasons: medical, energy and stamina, a desire to lose weight or change body shape. Whether you can't walk up a short flight of stairs without panting or are ashamed to put on a bathing suit, exercise will help you look and feel better. Notice, I did not say "be *perfect*"; I said, "look and feel *better*."

I have been involved in fitness for over thirty years, and I still love the feeling of accomplishment after exercise. I do it because I am not only burning calories but helping my heart, lungs, bones, and muscles get stronger. I have a clear understanding with myself as to *why* I exercise. It is critical that you reach the same understanding with yourself. What is your primary goal, and what motivates you to do the work to reach that goal?

Know your "why"! Keeping yourself motivated is most of the battle to a healthier, happier you. It is your motivation that enables you to tap into your inner athlete and stay on track when those unexpected challenges cause you to think about quitting. Along with that is staying in the present. I was a mess when I started to exercise, but I knew that exercise happens *now* — not tomorrow, not Monday, but *now*! Figure out the specific thing that motivates you to exercise, then keep it in the back of your mind all the time. Now. When you get the urge to quit, remind yourself *why* you started and exercise *now*.

Before you get started, be sure to check with a doctor or health professional to verify that there's no reason you shouldn't be starting an exercise program. If this is your first time to exercise, start off slow and gradually increase the duration of the workout. Make a well-thought-out plan. With a good plan, this journey will be so much easier; without a good plan, you are likely setting yourself up for failure or even serious injury. Exercise is a science, and it's a good idea to approach it that way. Your weekly exercise routine should include resistance training to build or maintain muscle and some form of aerobic exercise to improve your cardiovascular health.

If you have never worked out before, you might start with aerobic exercise. It requires very little time but a lot of effort, and studies suggest that it improves your cardiovascular and metabolic health. Take a class or use a *ShapelyGirl* fitness or another cardio DVD. Do what you can, start slow, and in weeks you will be amazed at what you have accomplished. Most people dread the thought of exercise, but as your life is changed for the better, you may never learn to love it, but you will know its value.

I have loved exercise from day one, but over time I have changed the kind of exercise I do. I love to teach fitness, but biking and power walking are my times for prayer and solitude (a great motivation). Moving is a part of my life, and it should be a part of yours. Can you give me thirty minutes a day for three days to begin? Are you worth it? Yes, you are, and you can do this!

Here are five tips to get you moving:

1. **Believe you are entitled to look and feel better.** Nothing makes you feel better than doing something good for yourself that will enable you to do something good for others. How many times have you heard, "When you take care of yourself, it is much easier to take care of those who depend on you." I am not the first to whisper this in your ear! Moving will help you have a positive attitude and motivate you to positively push forward. Moving daily will give you a feeling of personal freedom filled with happiness. Take a group fitness class, hire that personal trainer you've been thinking about, try a yoga or Pilate's class, and incorporate meditation and relaxation. Go to a day spa. All these things will help you connect with yourself while you look and feel better each day. You are worth it!

2. **Exercise relieves stress and depression.** In the next chapter, I will tell you about my breakdown and spending time in the psychiatric ward of a hospital. While I was there, I knew that one of the best remedies for depression was exercise. I announced to the other patients that I was going to give an aerobics class and invited them to join me. They showed up, I got in my grove, and we began to move. It was crazy, but it worked. The staff watched and saw the benefit, so I led a workout every day until I was released a week later. A fitness program helps lower blood pressure and bad cho-

lesterol, strengthens and tones muscles, and relieves stress and depression by releasing endorphins in the brain. Endorphins make you feel great and make it so much easier to work through the problems and challenges of life.

3. **Set goals and visualize your successes.** One of the problems people encounter when starting a new fitness program is having unrealistic goals they cannot attain. It is foolish to think you can run a marathon before you can even run a mile. Goals need to be realistic and achievable, or you will give up too soon. Short-term goals need to happen quickly and then be followed up with long-term goals. Have a plan and execute it; don't just fly by the seat of your pants and go any way the wind is blowing. Write down your plan, and be persistent when life gets in the way. Keep moving! I have had many setbacks, challenges, and mountains to move and still do. They may make me stop for the moment, but I refuse to let them define my life. I tell that voice that wants to quit or keep me down that I am in charge. Visualize reaching your goal and do not give up. Cut off the inner critic by saying, "I can and will do this thing." See yourself doing it and do it! Be steadfast and focused.

4. **Connect with positive people who can inspire you.** To make real changes in any area of your life, you need to have support. It is very hard to lose weight and get fit, so the last thing you need is more craziness from people who tear you down. Make new friends in exercise classes and support groups that will help you stay focused. I found a class with a nonjudgmental instructor, who was there to get

me through my workouts. Then I befriended like-minded women who supported me and I them. In fact, I started a Friday group for emotional eaters over thirty years ago. Every Friday, we would meet at my house for lunch and talk about our issues with food. I served them tuna salad with lettuce and tomato. Find a group that will encourage you and make you feel valued as you work toward your goals. Hire a trainer who will take the time to identify your needs and goals, then help you to achieve those goals.

5.  **Decide to let nothing get in the way.** Along your journey, you will encounter many obstacles that will push you to give up. The road of regular exercise is long and bumpy, and you must continually choose to keep the right perspective. Perseverance is part of creating change in your life. Sometimes it's easy to get discouraged. Believe me, years ago I was a walking billboard for it. I looked at everything with blind eyes and a broken spirit. Thank God, I got off my couch, climbed those stairs, and began to move. Then, when I found out this exercise journey wasn't always smooth sailing, I learned how to get past the roadblocks and keep going. You must decide that exercise is a life-saving priority that needs to be maintained.

Move. Breathe. Transform!

## 11

# Breaking Down

*I*n Colorado, I slowly dropped weight. As I became more fit from exercise, I also developed healthy eating habits. I loved my work with the Richard Simmons organization until it closed. I had made some monumental changes in my life. Although it looked like the primary reason was regular exercise and eating right, it was actually something that came as a total surprise.

I had an assistant named Trudy, who asked me to go to church every week, and every week I said no. She would smile and tell me that she and her family prayed for me. I had no idea what that meant, but I thought, *Okay. Can't hurt!* One week she asked, and I think I responded maybe, which she took as a yes. Low and behold, she showed up at my door that Sunday morning.

I decided to go. Maybe I would meet someone new at this Happy Church. Yes, that's what it was called! So, we walked into this big place, and I was checking out the guys. Nothing prepared me for what happened next. I had been used to going to boring masses, but this was spectacular. We took our seats in the first row of the balcony, but we didn't sit very long. There was a great band, and people began singing, waving their hands around, and even dancing. The atmosphere was so free, I was totally caught up in it.

The pastor was a woman named Marilyn Hickey, and she taught the Bible in a way I had never heard before. At the end, she asked if anyone wanted to come forward and receive Jesus as their Lord and Savior, and I literally felt God's Spirit overtake me. I didn't know what was happening. The next thing I knew, I was at the altar, crying and giving my life to Jesus.

I had heard about Jesus in the Catholic Church, and I had always believed in Him; but I had never surrendered my life to Him. As a result, I never really knew Him. After that encounter at the altar, I began to know Jesus as a real person, my very best friend, my savior, and the master of my life. I went to Happy Church and Bible studies. I had always known God was with me, but now I was experiencing His presence in a real, tangible way. The Bible was a new book to me also. I loved the psalms, where David would pour out his heart to God and be comforted.

There is a spiritual component of becoming whole, no matter who you are and what your traumas or negative experiences have been. You may choose a different way, but I was saved by Jesus. I read how He died a horrible death on the Cross because He loved me. He took my sin and all its consequences on himself so that I could get free of them. As far as I'm concerned, He hung on that Cross and said, "Father, forgive Debra. She doesn't know what she's doing." So true! Then, because Jesus forgave me and all my sins — past, present, and future — He helps me forgive others. That's a miracle!

I wasn't always faithful to Jesus, but He has always been faithful to me. His love is what really changed my life. I believe His love got me up those stairs and into that aerobics class. His love enabled me to leave dysfunctional relationships and try to find healthy ones. His love kept me moving, crushed the inner critic, and helped me eat good food for my body. Now, I was going to face the greatest pain of my life, and He would be there to comfort me and strengthen me all the way through it.

When my job with Richard Simmons was over, I moved back to Philadelphia. I got a job working at the fitness center at Graduate Hospital, where I met my good friend Elsa. During this time, I also met and married a strikingly handsome guy, who had a personality that was opposite of my exes. Instead of being controlling, abusive, and addicted, he was passive, unmotivated, and immature. He came from a wealthy family, where little had been expected of him. He was insecure in making decisions and utterly dependent on me. I earned the wages, cooked the meals, and called the shots. That Christmas, he gave chia pets to his family and Garfield slippers to me!

I was in my mid-thirties and began having nightmares. They were so vivid, I would wake up in the middle of the night sweating and hysterically crying for someone to rescue me. I felt the pull of my past, like something gnawing at me. My routine of healthy eating and daily exercise wasn't working for me any longer. At my all-time lowest weight, to the outside world it didn't look like there was anything wrong with me; but I felt anxious all the time, and my mind was starting to play tricks on me. I didn't know exactly what was happening inside my head, but I sensed I needed help.

I never told my husband about my past, as I never felt it was his business. Although I had always told people I had been abused as a child, I had never talked to a therapist. It didn't seem like a big deal to me. I thought this happened to all little girls. Besides, I couldn't remember all the details of what had happened to me. I behaved like the happy, positive woman I am today, but inside I was emotionally bound to the past.

With the mental and emotional tension building inside me, I began slipping. I felt like I had to get away from everything and everybody, including my new husband. After years of control, my past compulsion to eat was starting to weigh on me and the inner critic surfaced. It wasn't long before I saw no way out but binging. The self-destructive cycle started again.

One night, after working on my feet for almost twelve hours at an upscale restaurant, panty hose rubbing my thighs, I came home to find my husband watching cartoons. There was no food in the house, and my patience was at an all-time low. I huffed off to food shop. OMG, he was following me to the car to come with me! We were in the store at 9 p.m., I was grabbing whatever looked good, and he told me he wanted cereal. I told him to go and get it. The next thing I knew, he was calling me to help him pick out a box of cereal. "Should I get Rice Krispies or Frosted Flakes, or maybe Special K?" Then he wanted me to read the labels with him, to see what was the healthiest one.

I could feel my blood pressure rising and started to melt down in the cereal aisle. I tried to breathe, started to pant, and then lost it. I must have fainted, as the next think I knew, the paramedics were there with oxygen and a gurney. I was headed for the ER. That was it for me. It was time to run away again. The next day, I packed a suitcase and drove to my cousin's in Florida. She had a beautiful apartment and agreed to let me stay with her for a while. She had no idea what was going on with me, because I couldn't articulate it to her or anyone else.

The new scenery did little to help. I was spiraling down, and it was not a pretty. I binged, worked, slept as much as possible, and cried for the past I could not hide from anymore. I wrote each of my parents an eight-page letter, because I was thinking of taking my life. I was a failure. Both of my parents had abandoned me, my mother emotionally and my father physically. I felt I had no one. I did not even feel God. My grandmother was still alive, and she wanted me to come home, but the loneliness and hopelessness were too deep. I could not face anyone.

My weight escalated, and all I thought about was eating and death. Suicidal thoughts were worse by the day. This was the darkest season of my life. I was very close to death. I could feel it. The thought started to become a plan, and I decided to hang myself. I saw no other way out of the pain. Like a drunk on their last bender, I went to a bakery, bought a dozen doughnuts, and sat down to eat every one of them. People were watching me, and I could feel the shame, guilt, and darkness coming from them. With every bite, I saw myself getting fatter and fatter.

I headed back to my cousin's. Soon, I had a rope tied around my neck and was pacing back and forth. If you have never been depressed — really depressed — you have no idea what this degree of suffering is like. When someone kills themselves, I know that darkness. Depression is not feeling sad; it is like a pit you cannot crawl out of. No amount of money, status, or celebrity will stop it.

I did not worry that my cousin would come home and find me. That was not even a thought. I just wanted the pain to stop. However, in the end, I could not kill myself. Part of me wanted to, but something bigger stopped me. I truly believe there were angels all around me, protecting me. I credit divine intervention and the grace of God for being alive today.

Instead of hanging myself, I called a hotline, and they recommended a therapist. I called him, and he made me promise I wouldn't hurt myself before I met him at his office. Over the next couple of months, Glen helped me break out of that suicidal pit of despair. His was the hand I held onto to keep from drowning. He listened to my story and validated my experience without question. While describing what happened to me, I said, "When I had sex with Marsh," and he stopped me abruptly.

"Let's be clear about this. You didn't have sex with anyone. You were a child, who was violated by an adult." I was so grateful to him! For the first time in my life, I saw that the abuse was not my fault.

For the moment, I didn't want to die; but I still did not feel good. I do believe those angels continued to stay with me. I still believed God had his hand on my life and that I was meant to do something meaningful. I didn't know what that was then, but today I see that I was meant to live through those difficult times to help other women.

Glen worked with me week after week, and soon I felt better. I learned that what happened to me did not happen to all girls and my abusers were sick people. Realizing that the abuse was not my fault was the truth that began to liberate me. After a while, I was strong enough to go back to Philly, but I have never forgotten the work Glen did with me.

Back in Philly, things got worse before they got better. I divorced my husband and moved in with Elsa. We shared a tiny efficiency apartment with her dog, Mazel Tov. The three of us slept together on a futon! I went back to work at Graduate Hospital in the fitness center. I had times of screaming, crying, and having to relive the years of pain, as I was in treatment with both a psychiatrist and a psychologist. They were helping me to fully recover my memories.

The significance of the abuse was coming forward, and I was feeling sicker. In a way, therapy helped me break down. I was starting to mentally and emotionally slip out of reality again. I needed to acknowledge and accept the things that had happened to me, but to do that meant I had to face the monstrous events of my past. I wrote in my journal, "I decided to feel the pain."

My mind could no longer handle these destructive memories, and I began to unravel. Then I totally blanked out. I remember the day, place, and time like it was yesterday. I felt numb, and my thinking was skewed, until my mind went totally blank. I had become friends with a psychiatrist, whose office was in the same building as the fitness center, and I would stop in to see her regularly when I was working at the hospital. I don't know how she perceived those dark parts of my life, because I never was her patient. I can't remember if we discussed those secrets prior to my breakdown, but the day I totally lost it she was there for me. I walked into her office, crawled under one of her office chairs, and curled up in a fetal position. I wanted to be anywhere but where I was: in a downward spiral and moving fast.

From there, I was admitted to the psychiatry unit of Albert Einstein Hospital in South Philly, where I stayed for three weeks, thanks to Elsa. This was another major turning point in my life, and I am so grateful for it. I was in a unit that housed people with mental disorders ranging from depression and paranoid schizophrenia to transgender personality disorder. One guy was admitted in the middle of the night in restraints because he was hurting himself.

My floor had bars on the windows, lights on 24/7, and all patients' doors were open at all times. My roommate was a very elegant, mainline woman, who had also had a mental breakdown. She was always dressed like she was eating at the yacht club. She worked for an upscale accounting firm in Center City, and I would never figure out how anyone with that kind of life could wind up next to me. Nevertheless, Christine and I hit it off. She was about fifteen years older and was discharged before I was. I never saw her again, but I think of her often.

We were on the fourth floor, with people suffering from all kinds of mental and emotional problems, people from all walks of life. I heard screaming, crying, and people talking to themselves nonstop. It was always noisy, and sleep — even with meds — was impossible. There was no privacy with the doors open. I was fed a high fat, high sugar, and high salt diet. I sat all day in this scary place, knowing I couldn't just walk out the front door; I had to be discharged.

I had to get out. I realized that nobody knew where I was. The hospital wasn't allowed to tell anybody I was there, so I had to call people and let them know. I could use the pay phone, so I called my mother and told her where I was. I could hear her voice quivering, like she was going to cry. I had never seen or heard her cry. I felt sorry for her, as I felt I had caused so much chaos in her life.

As I mentioned before, I started leading regular exercise to help us all feel better. Then, my family was invited to a therapy session with the social workers, who had helped me tremendously. My mother, father, and brother came, but it was not what I expected. I think I expected to get rescued. My brother sat right next to the door, getting up to pace back and forth, looking like he was ready to run out. My father and mother began fighting and blaming each other for the failure of their marriage. My social worker stopped it and asked them all to leave. When they were gone, he said, "Well, that was useless."

This was the year Prozac, the anti-depressant wonder drug, was approved. It worked wonders for me. I was almost a new woman. Being able to think more clearly, I knew I never wanted to be here again. I desperately desired to get better, and I did. I no longer wanted to die; instead, I wanted to fight and get whole. While there, I learned about a women's sexual abuse survivor's group at Hahnemann Hospital that I could attend as an outpatient. It was a closed group, led by a well-known and respected therapist, who interviewed me and invited me to join. This was the real start of my recovery.

I had always thought that losing weight and becoming fit would fix me. Then I knew that God could fix me. But sometimes His way is not the easy street we think it will be. Sometimes you have to scrape the dung off the road and use it to fertilize the flowers. I had to become fully aware and face the reality of what I had been through. I had to see it for what it was, accept that it had happened, and understand that it wasn't my fault. I had to accept that my mother couldn't or wouldn't protect me. In the process of reliving and feeling my trauma and worst fears, I found out how strong I was. I love this quote form Eleanor Roosevelt: "You gain strength, courage, and confidence by every experience in which you really stop to look fear in the face. You must do the thing which you think you cannot do."

# 12

## Feeling the Pain

*W*ho would consciously choose to feel pain? It goes against every human instinct. For a child who was sexually abused, denial is a survival mechanism, especially when they have been threatened or intimidated into silence. To become a healthy adult, we need to come out from the shadows of our denial so we can heal? How can we go through the pain without it devastating us?

Denial is defined as a refusal to admit the truth or reality. While it does function as a means of protection for a while, suppressed memories start to emerge from our subconscious. This is good, because dealing with these memories and coming out of denial is the way to become whole. By my mid-thirties, the truth was there, waiting for me, wanting to set me free. My past was no longer avoidable. I had to work through the pain, which meant exposing my secrets instead of eating them away. No more secrets!

Trauma is a normal reaction to an abnormal situation. When reality becomes too much to bear, we protect ourselves by separating our mind from what our body is experiencing. We learn quickly how to "zone out." We go somewhere else in our minds to escape the physical reality of what is happening to our bodies. Psychologists refer to this as "dissociation."

Denial is one way the brain protects itself. When you are in denial, you stop connecting to your body, trusting your senses, or feeling appropriate emotions. This defense mechanism becomes a pattern that can follow you into adulthood and prevent you from fully enjoying your life journey. In a sense, you have shielded yourself from feeling pain but, at the same time, you have also weakened your ability to experience joy. You sleepwalk through life, mostly out of touch with reality.

Your body is a wonderful machine. It sends you signals of distress and contentment, anxiety and peace, grief and joy, hunger and satisfaction. Without recognizing those cues, you lose touch with the world around you. When you disconnect from your body, you lose the ability to experience the comfort and pleasure that it can provide, and you tend to ignore your instincts. For instance, you may no longer fully recognize situations or people that should make you fearful.

A woman dissociates from her body when it has not been a safe place in which to dwell. It has been violated and devalued, bruised her self-esteem, and constrained her ability to move with ease. She has been teased or rejected because of it, so it has caused emotional and physical pain. It is not hard to understand why she would want to disconnect from it. She lives in her head and leaves her body somewhere else.

We have been told by the media, Hollywood, and even those close to us that our larger bodies are unacceptable and proof of our moral weakness and lack of self-control. Our size and the criticism it brings make us feel less-than-human. We hate our bellies, hips, and legs. We stop looking in the mirror, as there is an attitude of, "Don't Look at Me — Don't See Me." There is a war against obesity, and we are the enemy.

We can almost be invisible to ourselves. This mindset makes it easy to retreat into *Fear, Food, and Fat.*

The body/mind disconnect is not unique to overweight women. It is experienced by women of all sizes. Maybe you feel that your authentic self is your thin self, to be reclaimed sometime in the future, when you finally reach your ideal weight. When your definition of healing is being thin and thinness is beyond your reach, then peace is only something that exists in your fantasy of the future.

"Don't tell," you were told, but maybe that was a long time ago. Maybe now is finally the time to get your secrets out in the open. Even though you are an adult, the notion of telling your family the truth about sexual abuse in your past is not easy. It can have unexpected and unpleasant consequences, sending shockwaves through a family. There is so much shame about this subject, the victim can potentially be blamed or simply not believed by family members who are more comfortable staying in a state of denial.

When secrets surface and are told, relationships are re-examined in uncomfortable ways. Questions may be asked about an enabling parent's role. Revealing your sexual abuse can wound an entire family as you uncover your wounds. The fact that you are on a healing journey does not necessarily mean everyone else wants to come along for the ride. You may receive support from some relatives, but you might not. It can be freeing to speak out, but it can also create a mess. That is one of the reasons it is so important to find care from a trained professional and a supportive community of people who understand what you are going through before you include your family in your recovery.

Jesus said in John 8:32, "And you will know the truth, and the truth will set you free." You need to face the truth, understand what happened to you, be honest with yourself, and speak openly about everything with a therapist, who can assist you in fully recovering your memories and addressing your shame. You must shine a bright light on those dark memories in a safe place. Once you tell the truth, you usually make better choices for yourself.

The desire to escape our pain limits our personal growth, continues a state of denial, and creates greater suffering down the road. However, deciding to come out of denial and face the truth may make you to feel worse before you feel better. You are basically choosing to face the truth and feel the pain, because that is the only way to expel the roots of that pain from your life. Try to think of the emotional pain in the same way you might view the pain after a vigorous workout. Healing from sexual abuse has the same "no pain, no gain" aspect as physical exercise, because it also brings the long-lasting benefits of making you a stronger person emotionally. You will be better able to deal with stress without triggering your food addiction, zoning out, or reliving your shame.

There are many paths to trauma: racism, sexism, death of a loved one, being bullied or teased. Any of these can be traumatic and result in the kind of shame that leads to many forms of addiction, including Binge Eating Disorder. If you look at your life through a lens of trauma, you may see things you never thought contributed to your eating disorder or other problems. A therapist will help you not to dwell on your pain or focus on the adversity you have faced. They will help you deal with the trauma, which will stop the self-blame and shame that cause the cycle of depression and addiction.

Focusing on eating — or dieting — rather than facing your pain adds to your pain. Peace comes when you stop trying to avoid the painful feelings. But you need the right support to do that without destroying yourself. It is hard work to recover the truth of what happened to you. Sometimes you must accept that the unthinkable is true. It may mean you will have flashbacks and lose control of your emotions for a while. Some of us grieve or hit bottom several times before realizing we are getting stronger.

When you finally understand that feeling the pain won't destroy you, it liberates you. Feeling the pain opens your life in ways you never imagined and is the beginning of accepting the truth of your past, living in the real world, and being fully conscious in the present. It is knowing the truth and living free of the effects of trauma.

Once you have made the choice to feel the pain, it is important to find a therapist who has been trained in treating trauma. There is growing awareness in the field of mental health of how important it is for survivors of sexual abuse to receive treatment by a professional who understands the aftermath of trauma. There are many treatment centers across the country that could refer you to a qualified therapist, who is specifically trained in treating Binge Eating Disorder. There is inpatient as well as outpatient care available for people suffering from BED. In addition to individual therapy, there are support groups you may find helpful. There are retreat houses offering recovery programs, and local hospitals may have group meetings for trauma survivors. As the poet Felicia Hemans wrote, "Strength is born in the deep silence of long suffering hearts; not amid joy."

If you are like me, by accepting your pain, your healing can begin:

1. You have been hurt.
2. You are a prisoner of your pain.
3. You can't go on like this another day.

If you are going to overcome the power of Binge Eating Disorder, you must find a new way of experiencing your life.

- Recognize your pain instead of avoiding it, defending or hardening yourself against it. Open your heart to it.
- Sit with your feelings and practice mindfulness.
- Allow the pain to define you in a positive way. You have overcome a lot.
- Feel pride in your strength, resilience, and ability to love deeply despite the abuse in your past.
- Find the vulnerable place inside you and offer yourself the same comfort and understanding you would offer a friend who was in pain.
- Find a way to return to this place in yourself so you can access it when you feel yourself returning to the call of your food addiction or the stress in your life.
- Offer comfort to others who are in pain. It can take you beyond the world of your own suffering and bring you peace.

What do you have to lose if you recover? What would you gain? It may sound absurd, but if you could sit face-to-face with your pain and talk to it, what would you say? What would you hear? What could your suffering tell you about yourself? What purpose has it served for you? What has it prevented you from doing or being? What would it feel like to say goodbye to it? There is a spiritual lesson inside your pain that could open you to great joy. Try to figure out what that lesson is and how to make the most of it.

We can choose to become fully aware of what is going on right now, in this moment of our lives, especially when difficult situations bring on distress. We can be mindful and overcome the compulsion to binge, to find comfort in something other than eating. This belief is at the heart of recovery and offers us the chance to find new coping mechanisms.

The transition from the old life to a new life is a period of limbo, where the past is too painful to return to and the future is too uncertain to feel comfortable about. There is much to be done, and it cannot be done all at once. If you plunge headlong into your wounds, you will be compelled to seek comfort and relief in the only way you know how — a return to your addiction of choice.

Again, this is the reason it is so important to accept that you cannot recover alone and must reach out to others for help. Reaching out for help with something as difficult as overcoming addiction means you are in the most emotional pain you have ever felt in your life. You are living in the bottomless pit. At the same time, your therapist and support group are encouraging you to give up the only comfort and relief you've ever known! The difference is that instead of using addiction to deny the trauma and avoid the pain of it, you are choosing to face the trauma and feel the pain of it. Ironically, this choice — as difficult and painful as it is — will stop the trauma from causing you pain.

Every day, you become stronger and the pain loses a little more of its hold on you. Then, one day, you realize you have lived an entire day without one thought or desire to binge, without one pang of guilt or shame, and you have felt a deep peace and joy about yourself and your life.

# 13

## "I Choose Me"

My mother ignored my escalating weight, but my extended family talked about nothing else. Meals and shopping were always about my weight. I remember my great aunt, Marion, telling me at a family dinner that God made food hot so we would eat slowly and enjoy the taste. I thought, *You want me to eat slow and taste the food?* Seriously, because compulsive eating has nothing to do with taste or pleasure. I never remember tasting the food. I ate to fill the hole in my soul.

Grandmother Viola loved me and wanted me to be like other kids, so she nagged me to lose weight. At every meal, she watched each morsel that went into my mouth. As I reached for seconds, she would ask, "Do you really need to have more food?" At the time, I felt she was belittling me, and it created great internal anxiety. The more she talked about my weight, the more I ate. At that age, I did not understand her intentions as I do now.

As a teen, my grandmother had my father drive me to every diet doctor in the region. I had pregnant cow's urine injected into me. I took diet pills. Before meals, I'd eat these little chocolate candies that were supposed to suppress my appetite. My jaw was wired shut. I did one of those "drink-three-shakes-a-day" fasting diets. After nothing but these shakes for weeks, I went on a binge. When my electrolytes went out of balance, I ended up in the hospital and almost died.

I didn't begin to reach my permanent weight until I stopped conventional dieting and silenced the inner critic. Getting to a healthy weight and maintaining it took a lot of time; it was not an overnight, instantaneous miracle. But it is still a miracle! Some miracles come through time, effort, and maintaining hope. Weight-loss takes commitment, dedication, focus, and a will to stand up when you begin to lose *hope*. My Christian faith gave me hope and strengthened me when I began to lose hope. You may get hope from something else, but we all need that spiritual component. Every now and again we lose sight of our goals, and we need someone greater than ourselves to hold onto our *hope*, or we will have nothing. My losing weight and keeping it off is a miracle because I didn't do it in my strength; when I was weak, I prayed and God gave me His strength.

In this way, I worked very hard to stay focused on my goals and get off the mental roller-coaster ride. I still do today. It was all worth the success I enjoy now. Do I feel accomplished? You bet I do! I have learned how to eat what I want. If I overeat, I tell myself I did it, I own it, and I will refuse to judge or loathe myself. I stopped that self-abuse for good. When I tell women to eat what they want, they laugh at me. They'll say, "For you, that works; but I am addicted to food." Really? I ate out of trashcans and hid food under my bed, remember?

Over the years, I have been asked this one question again and again: "How long did it take you to lose 150-plus pounds?" I can't say exactly, but if I think it was about three years. The first thing I did was read everything I could on nutrition, but the articles were scarce and very scientific. There was no Internet, and if you wanted to find out about good nutrition, you asked bodybuilders. They would say, "Lots of protein, and stay off the carbs." It was not that simple, but early on they were the go-to crowd. I would observe skinny people, and almost all of them just didn't eat much.

There were many challenges, setbacks, and off days, but I always managed to restore my hope and visualize the finish line. How could I do this? One of the reasons was because my goal had radically changed. No longer was my hope set on the goal of being skinny and perfect; my goal was set on the hope that I could feel normal and love myself the way God loved me. Losing weight gave me some confidence, but I needed to love myself unconditionally, like He did. Then I would be fully confident that I was worth it, that I deserved to feel great. In that sense, I chose me.

I didn't always like it when people said I looked good. Years ago, after losing weight on a diet, someone noticed and said I looked good. That created tremendous anxiety. I was not used to getting compliments and didn't think I was worthy of them. Not knowing how to deal with them, I would eat from anxiety and regain the weight. I did not want to be noticed, because I did not love myself. I was not emotionally ready to receive a compliment. Until I crushed that inner critic by learning to love myself, I remained hidden.

Everyone wants a quick, weight-loss solution, but it is a daily choice to keep on track and refuse to give up, even when you stumble. I chose me because my life depended on it, and that made me relentless. I was not going to give up or give in again. I needed to keep moving forward and not give in to the pressures I felt from family, friends, society, and my old thinking. I took my time, and today I feel and look better than ever. I have had my weight off over twenty-five years. There were so many times I wanted to give up, but the alternative looked bleak — and I was not going back there. You must take the time you need and choose you!

For years, I have worked with women desperate to lose weight, hearing and empathizing with their pain and longing to look and feel better. The majority (close to all of them) were on some sort of diet. I'm not talking watching what you eat but drastically altering their lives by going on a fad diet to lose weight quickly. These diets capitalize on our fear of being fat and desire for instant results. Many have little scientific basis or proof of long-term success, nor are they medically safe.

Calorie-restricting diets drastically lower your metabolism, putting your body into starvation mode. When this happens, you begin to store fat and lose lean muscle mass. You do not burn the fat that is holding you captive, and you promote an unhealthy cycle of eating. You need to eat to strengthen muscles and burn fat, especially when exercising regularly.

Diets are promoted on the testimonies of people who are paid to try the products and have gotten fast results. Watching any diet commercial is almost nauseating to me now. Listening to every psychologically scripted word lures you to pick up the phone and make that call out of sheer desperation. "Do this now! You can lose ten pounds for ten dollars a month" — says a celebrity who is compelling. She is the girl next door. She gets your pain. She gets you. She makes you believe she has your best interest at heart. She is the newest queen of diets.

These celebrities have made us believe their diet — their way — is the answer for us. They say, "I lost my weight, and so can you!" But it is business. They are making money by capitalizing on their weight loss, and many of them put it right back on. Diets are all about their way not yours. Someone else tells you what to eat and think. You choose diets because you do not trust yourself to make the right decisions. The diet chooses the "right" food, portion, and times to eat.

How do they know that their way is right for you? What is right for me may not be right for you. This is key, because we all function at different metabolisms and energy levels. What works for me may not work for you. I might have breakfast for dinner and little snacks the rest of the day. You may have three meals and nothing else. What is the right way to eat? Time to figure out what is best for you. Get in touch with what your body needs. A diet's "right" way to eat may have nothing to do with what your body needs!

I got off the dieting cycle of frustration and failure when I began to value and respect myself, to trust myself to find out what my body needed and then feed my body accordingly. I began the great adventure of discovering what foods made me more energetic and happier and what foods made me feel bloated, tired, and wanting more. I discovered when were the best times for me to eat and how much of each food. This did not happen overnight, but I was persistent. As I figured out what worked for me, my whole view of food changed. I turned from choosing diets to choosing me.

Let me encourage you to begin to look at this as an experiment to figure out your body's needs and get yourself to a better place in the process. When I first began do this, I cut my portions in half. Instead of losing weight, I put on a pound here and there and was totally discouraged. I wanted to give up, but I was determined to figure it out. I learned that eating healthy doesn't decrease weight overnight. The body adjusts and weight fluctuates. You can weigh two to three pounds heavier at night than you do in the morning.

Stay focused on the journey and never allow judgment or shame in this process. Take the time to experiment, and eventually you will understand a new way of eating that will help to nourish and satisfy. After failing at so many diets, you may find it hard to trust yourself, but I did and you can too. Allow yourself to fail until you succeed. Don't give up, because you are worth it!

I gave a lecture at the University of Pennsylvania Hospital for weight loss surgery clients. At the end of the lecture, I opened the floor to questions and comments. One woman's comment I will never forget. She had had gastric bypass surgery, and this was her first-year anniversary. She said she had met a woman who had told her she never had had an eating problem nor dieted, so she asked her, "When you open a bag of M&M's, when do you stop eating?"

The other woman replied, "When I am full. When do you stop eating?"

She said she answered, "When the bag is empty."

As a compulsive eater, eating half or part of anything was never an option. I was never satisfied until it was gone. I never trusted myself enough to save all of it or part of it for another time. As I began to trust me and my inner critic lost control, as I found what worked and what didn't work for me, I began to eat better and feel better. But I had to continually remind myself that I was no longer interested in instant gratification or instant results; I was in this to be healthy and stay healthy.

Building trust in yourself will take time. It took time to reach rock bottom, and it will take time to climb out of the dark hole into the light of trusting and re-inventing yourself. Trust your decisions about what, when, and how much to eat. Let your body communicate the need. Give yourself permission to eat the "bad" foods, and eventually they will lose their power over you. Think positively, and keep reminding yourself that you can do this.

The pressure to be thin in this society is tremendous. Celebrities are expected to be size zero. In Hollywood, a size six is chubby. The media is brutal to any famous person who gains weight. They love publishing a front-page photo of a fat celebrity, ideally in a bathing suit. The average American woman is a size twelve to fourteen, and normal women are not often portrayed in the media. If we are honest, most of us would like to be thin. To come down from my 300-plus pounds, I had to change my view of what was truly desirable from the celebrity model to the normal, healthy model.

I stopped seeing dieting as the way to get there. It always went the same way, with me saying, "This time it will be different." But it was never different. I could never stick with the diet, and I regained more weight than I had lost. Finally, I figured, "Well, it's time to get back to real life, because dieting is not part of the real world." I had to learn how to eat properly and work through the emotional issues that were driving me to overeat and binge. I began to choose a healthy, normal me.

Women often do not want to listen when I tell them that restriction, starvation, and fast weight loss lead nowhere. The 100-billion-dollar-a-year diet industry has worked hard to get us to believe otherwise. That sales pitch worked on me for years, but eventually I realized the pattern of failure. When I became physically active and let go of the dieting mentality, I found the right path and personal peace.

I started with a good first meal and did not starve all day. I can't tell you how many overweight women have said they skipped breakfast entirely. They would wait until they were absolutely starving and then eat an enormous lunch. "Well, I skipped breakfast, so I'm entitled to splurge on lunch." In my case, I always feared that the first bite of the day would make me eat all day, but that did not happen once I changed my *mindset*. There is your key: *Stay in touch with **you** not the food*. You must talk with yourself, telling yourself that *you* can do this; it is only food and has no power or control over *you*. Silence the inner critic and change the conversation to your benefit. Even if you do not believe it, just do it.

When I stopped beating myself up for my imperfections and began to nurture myself, I became more and more free from the control of food. For the first time in my life, food did not dictate my days; I did. I have kept a journal for many years, keeping track of my progress in meeting various goals and keeping myself accountable to live my values. And, I pray daily, reminding myself that God loves me and I can love me just the way I am. I can choose me because He chooses me!

I pretty much ignore celebrity culture and their standards of what makes a woman beautiful. I get manicures and massages, because investing in my appearance and pampering my body encourages me to make healthier choices out of respect for my body. Most days, I plan what I am going to consume, allowing myself treats if I want them. I rarely deny myself any food, as that causes anxiety. It is not being mindful that usually leads me to binge.

Mindfulness is being conscious of what is happening right now. Mindfulness requires that you are open to your present experience. You pay attention to what is going on in the moment, listening to and accepting your body, having the courage to feel your emotions — not zoning out — and paying attention in a nonjudgmental way.

I practice positive self-talk to silence the inner critic and address what I'm thinking and feeling in that moment. When an emotion or a thought comes up that encourages me to eat, I say, "In God's strength, you are more powerful than any food. You are not going to allow food to overpower you." That might sound crazy, but it works!

When I make the right choice and eat healthy, I feel so much better. The pioneer in nutrition and health, Adele Davis, said, "We are indeed much more than we eat, but what we eat can nevertheless help us to be much more than we are." There is no doubt in my mind that this is true. Learning how to eat wisely was half the battle in becoming whole.

As I have said before, diets don't make you whole. You will need to educate yourself in what a balanced food program looks like, focusing on the importance of your good health, which will include weight loss. Moving your body must be a priority. When you understand good nutrition and the benefits of exercise, you will make better choices.

Ideally, you should work with a nutritionist who knows your history and can help you create a plan that feeds your hunger, keeps your trigger foods under control, and allows you to begin to build a healthy body. Try to give up boxed, processed food. Making these significant changes to your diet should also be done under medical supervision. There are treatment centers across the country that offer inpatient and outpatient programs for compulsive eaters. They provide you with guidance and support as you stop compulsive eating. This way, you do it safely.

I went to clinician after clinician, to weight management programs and eating disorder programs for specialized diets. I believed that if I could get my weight down, then everything was going to fall into place. I finally found a clinician who challenged that belief and made me do the important work that changed my life.

Recovery is a journey involving the twists and turns of life. You must learn techniques to cope with the daily challenges and any feelings of loneliness, anxiety, or sadness. Recovery does not mean you will never again eat emotionally, but you will form new habits to handle those times with inner peace instead of confusion and self-criticism. You will choose you over all other destructive thoughts and behavior.

Years ago, I had a conversation with a friend's daughter. I had not seen her in years, and she had lost a lot of weight on a diet only to gain it back plus more. She thought that because I had lost weight and kept it off, I had it all together. Not so! I still had the desire to binge at every emotion that haunted me. I was just learning how to control these emotions so that they could not sabotage my health. I told this young woman that I took one day at a time. I might have looked thinner, but my mind still could see me as fat if I let it.

Those of us who have had to break the habit of coping with trauma and difficult situations in life by eating will probably never totally lose our desire to comfort ourselves with food; however, we can dramatically improve our lives. Episodes of eating out of pain or discouragement will become less and less frequent, and we can let go of self-blame when we stumble and get back on track. We know how to eat to live in a healthy way, feeding our hunger rather than our emotions.

I will say this again and can't stress it enough: While there are many things you can do yourself to try to break the cycle of emotional eating, you need support. Professionals who specialize in treating trauma and eating disorders can help you in identifying the things that trigger binges. With their help, you can develop ways to avoid eating compulsively and mindlessly. They can assist you in feeling less threatened by things that happen to you or are said to you. You can discover what you really need and want. Then you can recognize your options and respond to a stressful situation by choosing a path that makes you feel happy in the long run. Life for anyone is hard, so professionals, pastors, girlfriends, family, and the God of your understanding are the support you need to turn any bad attitude or negative emotion around and stay on course or get back on course. They remind you, "We are meant to be whole not perfect."

The emotional damage you have suffered from abuse creates a false self. Your pain and addiction are not who you really are. The version the world sees, the person you pretend to be, is not who you really are. All these personas are imposters. As you recover and strip away the false personas, you might ask, "Who am I, really? If I'm not my trauma, my addiction, or the fake self I present to the world, who am I?"

Although the traumas of sexual abuse and obesity have been terrible, dealing with these problems has brought me to a great place of understanding and loving myself as well as others. Recovery from anything negative in life means finding your true self, the person you were meant to be. The process can be scary, but the rewards are amazing! It is worth it.

Discovering *you* is worth it. It can be frightening to be an adult, stripping away the lies, wondering what will be left after the pain and addiction are gone. The wonderful part of, "Who am I?" is that you are involved in redefining yourself. You get a "do-over." Through recovery and self-care, you discover a new set of tools to construct an authentic life. You will be the real you, free from compulsive eating, secrets, and shame. You will discover your true self.

When you open yourself to receive help and start to make changes, you retrain your brain. Your support system helps solidify the lifestyle changes, so that they become permanent. In a safe way, you share with others the things that you have kept secret. You speak about your pain. You embrace your spirituality. The wounds begin to heal, and your true self emerges. You may even uncover new talents and find a new reason for living.

Binge eating was a misguided way of providing compassion for your wounded self, but as you gain a healthier understanding of your past, you find healthy ways to receive comfort. You trade self-indulgence for self-care. Self-care says, "I am worthy. I invest in myself by respecting my body, adopting healthy lifestyle practices, managing stress, developing my spiritual life, and helping others in need."

Here are some tools to help you:

**Self-care** offers us healthy ways of coping, enhances our lives, and deepens our human experience. Nobody can make the decisions that need to be made to walk the road of recovery except us. Our parents are no longer in charge. Our spouses can't fix us. Diets don't work. God will help us, but He can't do anything until we decide to take that first step of faith.

Self-care means we don't put ourselves last on the list. We must find a way to handle our responsibilities to our families and jobs while fulfilling our commitment to be well and stay well. Without our health, mental and physical, we are of little use to anyone else. Self-care is vital to becoming whole.

Self-care is not pampering, like getting a spray tan or eyelash extensions. Self-care involves hard work and discipline. It means choosing behaviors that bring comfort and balance instead of falling into old, destructive habits. Our new, healthy activities should provide healing for our soul. We may not fully understand why or how all these things soothe us, but we know they do.

**Prayer** is an open dialogue with God. It is a way to express gratitude and to let him know that you see him at work in your life. Prayer allows us to reach the deepest part of ourselves and express humility, ask for forgiveness, seek guidance, and set goals. God reminds us that we are never alone and always loved. Regular communication with him reminds us that we are part of him and elevates our experience as human beings.

Those who pray regularly have a greater sense of purpose and receive more strength and faith to carry it out. They suffer less depression and recover from it more quickly. There are studies that show that people who pray tend to have shorter hospitalizations after surgery. People recovering from addictions find great healing from this connection to God, whatever their religious beliefs.

**Meditation** is recognized as one of the best ways to reduce stress. You quiet your mind and body so that healing can take place. Meditation is a mental discipline that takes you to a state of deep relaxation. Your mind is calm but completely alert. I love meditating on verses of Scripture that comfort me. Whatever form you choose, the goal is to calm your mind to attain inner peace or even an experience of the divine. Among the health benefits of mediation are lower oxygen consumption and an increase in serotonin production, which relieves anxiety.

**Journaling** is a useful tool to record your thoughts and feelings without judgment. Writing can be an outlet to release the emotion you might once have addressed by eating. It is a document of your journey in dealing with compulsive eating and your life experiences. Writing about your problems helps you to understand them and yourself in them. Journaling also can change your mood and make you feel more confident. Try recording what makes you proud, what makes you feel safe, what you are grateful for, and what your mission in life is.

**Gratitude** is a feeling of thankfulness for your life. It means acknowledging the gifts you have been given. Many women have talked about how valuable their gratitude journals have been in their lives. When you view life through a filter of appreciation, you begin to see that even on your worst days, something wonderful usually happens. When you are watching for it, you'll be surprised how often this is the case. Gratitude helps to retrain your brain to be more hopeful and to see challenges as opportunities. You can enrich your life by reflecting on how grateful you are for everything that makes your life precious.

**Body care** is an investment in yourself and a way of reconnecting your mind, body, and spirit. Believe you are entitled to look and feel better. Looking and feeling good is your right. When you take good care of yourself, you are better able to take care of everyone and everything else.

Even if you work from home, do your hair and makeup, get dressed. Treat yourself to a manicure, a massage, or a facial. Not only does body care make you look better, but you will feel better too. Take the time to relax and enjoy it. Turn off the cell phone, forget about your bills and your family; this time is for you. It is part of respecting your body and putting yourself at the top of the list.

Body care creates momentum to make more positive choices and changes.

**Massage** and other therapies have been shown to be very effective in treating trauma, including sexual abuse. We can contain trauma within our bodies even years after a traumatic event. The body creates a kind of tension to hold our pain, but that causes depression, disconnection, an extreme dislike of the body, and even physical pain. Massage and other kinds of bodywork therapies help release stored trauma, teach the body how to relax, help reclaim self-trust and respect, and enable you to feel more energetic.

**Nutritious eating** means eating for good health, to offer your body the energy it needs and your mind the proper fuel to be mentally alert. It does not mean "sticking to your diet." Not only does our mood affect how we eat, but how we eat affects our mood. Sugar and refined carbohydrates are our worst enemies. Particularly as we get older, we process food differently and have more trouble shrugging off toxic food. Therefore, women should do everything they can to avoid processed food and eating at fast-food restaurants, where even the so-called healthy choices aren't so good.

Eating a healthy amount of protein, vegetables, fruit, and fiber provides what your body needs. Make changes over time. Start with a healthy breakfast and go from there. Keep a food diary and make sure to record the way you are feeling physically each day. You may identify foods that trigger fatigue, depression, or inflammation.

**Positive self-talk** is what you do to combat the inner critic inside your head. This voice can seem very loud, especially for women working to recover from an eating addiction. Negative self-talk includes:

- Self-criticism: "I'm so stupid. I am fat and disgusting."
- Hopelessness: "I'll never succeed. I'll never recover from compulsive eating. I wasn't meant to be happy. I'll never find someone to love me."
- Anxiety about the future: "I'll lose my job, and then we'll lose the house."
- Perfectionism: "I'll never be happy if I'm not thin. I broke my diet, so I might as well eat whatever I want."

Learn to silence the inner critic with positive self-talk that includes a specific response to each negative statement. "I'm so stupid" should be countered with something like, "I am intelligent. I am capable. Everyone makes mistakes sometimes, and I can overcome this." There is research showing that when negative self-talk is eliminated, depression decreases. We cannot control everything in our lives, but we can control our thoughts. You can say no to every critical thought. You can surround yourself with positive affirmations, "Nobody and nothing has power over my mind, because I am in control of my thoughts. I decide to believe the truth and reject the lies."

**Group sharing and support** can be anything from online communities to just talking to a friend, who will listen without judgment. I had "circle time" after my fitness classes, where women could share their experiences and encourage each other. You invite others to witness your life and you witness theirs. You become more honest about your eating. You learn to speak from your heart. You find you are not alone in your struggles, and you can heal as part of a caring community. Your compassion for yourself and others deepens, and the group helps you to face your life one day at a time.

> *Where do I begin …? I have always been a plus-size girl who struggled with her weight. It soon became a part of my life that I never gave much thought to and just accepted. Everyone was not meant to be the same size, so I became a plus size "diva." I became this imaginary person that I did not like. I was fashionable, outspoken, and funny. I made everyone feel comfortable even though I was not comfortable with myself. There*

*was nothing I wouldn't do to prove to other people that I was not a typical "big girl." I was at a point where I was prepared to die young from being overweight, and I would marry someone who was in love with big women.*

*The wake-up call came when I developed a condition called polyostotic fibrous dysplasia, which produces too much insulin in the pancreas and causes fertility issues. I also had high blood pressure and was at 450 pounds. Still, there was nothing I thought could be done, because I felt I could not lose weight. But God said, "I have a different plan for you."*

*One day, while looking up activities to do in Philadelphia, I came across ShapelyGirl Fitness, which was offering a weight loss support group. I thought this might be something to help me get on my journey of losing weight. I called, and Debra Mazda picked up the phone. When she said hi and told me to come in the next day, I felt an instant connection. Still, I was very hesitant about going because I thought this was not going to be any different from groups I had tried in the past.*

*I was greeted with friendly smiles and a hug. No one looked at my size or made me feel like I was not welcome. Debra offered not only support groups, but nutritional shopping and healthy cooking habits – and the best of hugs and smiles to keep you encouraged. My group of women went through everything with me, and I have developed so many friends on this journey, which made it so much easier. Since I made that call, my life has not been the same.*

— *Sandy*

These are amazing tools that will help you find your balance in life. Then you can experience the lasting joy of health and well-being. And, like me, you can help others find the strength to say, "I choose me."

# 14

## Chained to the Scale

For years, I was shackled to my scale, measuring every ounce of self-worth and self-esteem by numbers that flashed back at me. Weighing myself only pulled me toward an emotional meltdown or a false high, as I associated my weight with being a bad or good person. I was scale obsessed, always feeling out of control and weighing myself numerous times daily. Like many overweight women, I would move the scale to a different floor, get on and off to see if the numbers went lower, and then vowed I would do better tomorrow.

I was consumed with my weight at the expense of things that really mattered, like relationships, my education, and a career. I allowed the number on the scale to become the way I measured success or failure. Week after week, I would say, "When I reach that number, I will do this. When I weight this, I can do that." Till then, I isolated myself from friends and all the things I could have been doing. I was fixated on the ideal number of pounds some doctor or professional told me I should weigh.

I was in the clutches of dieting, counting calories, and letting those numbers dictate my self-worth and self-confidence. Obsessing about these numbers — calories and pounds on the scale— contributed to the vicious and dangerous cycle of unhealthy eating rituals. As I have said before, somehow I got the courage to honestly evaluate my life and begin the healing process of recovery. I realized that my worth as a human being and a woman had nothing to do with my weight.

Over time, with many conversations and a lot of journaling, I began to change my thinking. I stopped obsessing over every pound. I learned there was power in giving up my scale and not counting every calorie. I no longer felt the need to measure every mouthful, worrying what my scale would say, how it would judge me. The scale and the calorie counter were not my judges! It was so freeing to be the commander of my ship. All these years later, I still feel the same way.

Periodically, I get weighed, but the scale is no longer my god. I am no longer a slave to it. I will also check the calories and read the labels on foods, but all this is simply a fact-finding mission. I make the decisions. I choose what I eat, how I exercise, and my attitude in any given moment.

Did you know that the number on your scale is a measurement of your body's water, fat, bones, and tissue in relation to the earth you stand on? You may not want to hear this, but no number on your scale will make you healthy, happy, or successful. Desperately, obsessively trying to reach that magic number causes you to do just the opposite. Obsessed with numbers, you neglect everything in your life that might give you a sense of well-being: getting your head straight, developing good relationships, finding and pursuing your purpose in life, and just having fun.

Getting weighed daily can be a trigger to feel shame, binge, or even be suicidal if the number isn't up to your standard. Realize that what you give your attention to is what can affect and even rule your life. You must trust yourself — not your scale. Choose to put your attention on people and things that really matter. That's why I encourage you to get up and get moving, to exercise. This is one activity that matters. It is something that enriches your life.

Body weight is a dynamic and fluctuating number. It is influenced by a variety of factors, such as stress, water intake, and illness. It's not just what you eat. Stop listening to what the world dictates and figure out what you need, what works for you. You need wisdom on how to eat for *you*, not what your next-door neighbor or some commercial says you need. Listen to your body rather than your scale.

An easy lie you can believe by reading magazines, watching TV, or surfing the Internet and social media, is that the number on your scale reflects how healthy you are. My weight can fluctuate while I still feel good and am healthy. And my weight is just how much I weigh at that moment. My health and well-being today are wrapped up in helping others as a fitness professional, exercising, eating to live, and having a great time in life. Again, the number on my scale is only my weight at this moment, and it will be different in hours or days. It doesn't judge me for yesterday or dictate what I do today or tomorrow.

If you are obsessed with the numbers on your scale, I encourage you to ditch it, at least for a while. Put it in the back of a closet or up in the attic, a place that will require some effort to get it. Turn your attention to nurturing and nourishing you. A healthy person eats a variety of foods, moves their body in a way that feels good, and finds joy and pleasure in self-care and caring for others.

I know you might be terrified to give up your scale. It can give you the false impression that you are in control. Let me tell you the truth: Giving up this toxic relationship with your scale will set you free! When I stopped weighing myself repeatedly, I began to focus and have the time and energy for things that mattered. I began to find my purpose in life and experienced joy, creativity, and happiness.

No longer will the scale set your mood for the day or determine what you will or will not accomplish. It will not stop you from exercising or make you ditch your greens. It can't say anything if it is not there! Only after you have established new habits of positive self-talk, good nutrition, and an exercise program — over a good amount of time — can you bring back your scale; and you bring it back only as a fact-finding tool. You are the boss not it.

Your self-esteem and worth as a woman is now based on the truth: You are a unique, gifted, compassionate human being. God loves you, others love you — and you love them and yourself. Every day is a new adventure in your journey to be healthy, happy, and successful in all you do. When things don't go your way, you refuse to give up. You fight for your health and wonderful life. No longer chained to the scale and addicted to food, you are totally committed to the noble cause of making a positive difference in your world.

## 15

# My Mother's Shadow

*A*fter my mother's death, I was going through old pictures and found a Christmas photograph of her, my brother, and me. My mother was looking at me, and her blank expression made me cry. The picture revealed her lack of feeling for me. I remembered years ago, while in an altercation with her, she calmly told me she would have aborted me if abortions had been legal then. I became hysterical and called my father. That was the first time I ever had had a conversation with him about her, and I was in my forties!

My father said, "Your mother was no good. She was morally weak and a terrible mother. You don't have to allow that to destroy you." After years of being sober from food, I went on a binge that night. I told myself that I needed to be soothed, and food had never let me down. But I didn't check out like I used to. I didn't run from the pain. I asked myself, *Who was this woman who gave birth to me?*

What drove my mother to close her eyes while I was being abused right under her nose? On some level of forgiveness, could I be compassionate towards her? I was not about to let her off the hook, but I wanted to understand. I began to talk ask God to show me, to help me remember things she had said to me, and I talked to relatives. This helped me put as much of the puzzle together as possible.

My mother was unmarried and pregnant at eighteen. In the 1950's, that was considered scandalous. She came from an Irish/Italian Catholic family of nine kids, and she was the second oldest. It was common for the older kids to look after the younger kids, and she complained that she had no freedom. They lived in a small row house, and all she wanted was to get out. She admitted to me that she got pregnant with me to escape. While I would be her ticket out, it also meant the end of her youth and the loss of any freedom she might have had as a single woman with no children.

My father married my mother, and seven months later I was born. They were a good-looking couple. My father was very handsome, and my mother was stunning; but we were far from a normal family. I would watch *Leave it to Beaver* and dream of being in the Cleaver family. I wanted to live with Ward and June Cleaver and have Beaver and his brother Tony as my siblings. They seemed so perfect. I had fantasies of my mother being home in an apron, cooking, and my dad coming home from work. We would all have dinner together. Reality was quite different. I never saw my parents kiss or hug, nor did I feel any love between them. I thought that if they could not love each other, how could they love me? This broke my heart.

I vaguely remember my dad living with us, as they separated early on. My grandmother told me that while they were separated, my father came over, and that was when my brother was conceived. Shortly after that, Marsh came on the scene. He may have kept my father away from my mother, but he certainly didn't protect me or my brother. Nor was he the father figure we needed.

Since my parents were separated most of my childhood, I never questioned why they got divorced. I am not sure how I felt about it, and no one asked me. Then my mother received a letter from St. Monica's Church, the parish where we lived, telling her the monsignor wanted to meet with her. I was still in elementary school, but she needed reinforcement, so she took me with her.

Neither of us had any idea why she was called to meet with the priest. My mother was told to meet him in the back pew of the church. As we walked in, there was complete silence. I could hear us breathing. I looked around and saw pictures of angels and saints, the confessional box, and the altar was lit up. There were candles burning everywhere. I had never been in the church except during mass. Now it seemed so peaceful, and I knew God was there with us.

We took holy water, made the sign of the Cross, and knelt at the pew. As we walked toward the middle of the pew, I asked God to comfort my mother. I sensed my mother's anxiety and felt like something bad was going to happen. While we waited, I took her hand to give her comfort. What could this possibly be about? As the rectory door opened, we saw our parish priest. He walked toward us, knelt at the pew, and made the sign of the Cross. As he approached us, my mother began to breath heavily.

He sat down, introduced himself, and made some small talk. Then he turned to us, and with his arm hanging behind the pew, he told my mother she was no longer welcome in the church. He said that the church did not welcome divorced people. My mother never said a word or questioned him. I think she was taken off guard and was embarrassed.

My heart sunk. How could this be? Did I hear him correctly? I wanted her to say something. *Plead with them to let you stay! Say something!* Not a peep. She just accepted the church's doctrine. This was our parish, where I attended elementary school, and now they were kicking her out. She would have no mass, communion, or penance. Where would I get married? Where would I baptize my children?

I was angry at the church for treating her this way. How dare they! They had no right. They were not God. They were just men who were sinners themselves. The Jesus I knew was loving and welcoming, which is what the Catholic Church taught me in religion classes at my Catholic school.

Being kicked out of the Catholic Church was just another point of pain for my mother and thus for me. She could be moody at times, and I received her wrath over any discomfort in her life. Because of me, at a young age she had become a single parent at a time when getting pregnant while not married *and* divorce were obviously frowned upon. I am certain she loved me on some level, but always on her terms. She had a love-hate relationship with me, probably because, on some level, she held me responsible for all her problems in life.

She worked hard and long hours as a waitress and seemed to love it. She rarely took a day off. This was most likely her relief from a life with two small kids and no husband to help. And, as I said before, she put her trust in money and was determined to make as much as possible. Sometimes she was my best friend and other times my worst enemy. I had a very insecure childhood, always guessing how she felt about me.

I had many cousins, so I spent a lot of my childhood with my mother's family. Holidays were always at one of my aunts' houses, and those are wonderful memories. All our family get-togethers were big, noisy affairs, with lots of food. Mostly, I loved being with my family. When the Beatles landed in America in the 1960's, all of my family watched *The Ed Sullivan Show* on my mother's black and white TV.

I was screaming when the door of the plane opened. There they were, the cutest boys I ever did see. I think I was about eleven years old. I was grateful my mother had a large family.

I didn't tell any of my family how angry I was with the church, and I was angry until Jesus helped me forgive and move forward. The guilt must have overwhelmed my mother as she continued to mail the weekly offering envelopes until I got older. Every time I saw her do it, my wrath boiled. I really had to fight my anger during college, when my neighbor across the hall had an affair with a Catholic priest and told me she was trying to get pregnant. Other neighbors welcomed the same priest every Friday for cocktails, and cocktails they had. I would hear them partying and think, *And you threw my mother out!*

I was also angry at my mother for divorcing and not trying to stay married. I was angry at a father who was never around, and I have very few and very vague memories of him. I was angry because my parents never realized how their actions affected me. I felt people's judgment and suffered rejection from the other kids.

My mother always wanted me to call her by her first name! And, she never used her married name, even when she was married to my father; so, her last name and our last name were always different. That was traumatic enough, but then the divorce marked me as a damaged kid. I lashed out at her and once told her that she had ruined my life.

By the time the priest told my mother she was not welcome in the church, I was ready to eat and eat a lot. Then my mother brought Marsh into our house, the abuse began, and I was totally lost in compulsive eating. Food was my coping mechanism and escape from reality. Obviously, I couldn't turn to my church for help. I stayed until I graduated high school, and then I turned my back on the Catholic Church for good.

My father's side of the family was Italian, and he was an only child. His mother, Grandmother Viola, was the real mother figure in my life. I have already described how much of my childhood was spent with her and Grandfather Joe. I stayed with them for weeks at a time and never wanted to go home. Grandmother Viola and I had many conversations. I was her life, probably the daughter she never had. She and my grandfather were very protective of me and the only ones I could rely on. I believe they kept me from becoming totally insane.

Grandpop was my hero. He loved to play cards at the union hall. He dressed up and always smelled so good. He wore hats and sang all the songs Frank Sinatra and Andy Williams sang, especially "Moon River," which he sang to me constantly. I think of him every time I hear it.

When Grandfather Joe died in 1969, part of me died too. He was still so young. He had a heart attack while he was at the union hall playing cards. I was devastated; the man I loved was gone. Now it would be me and my grandmother. After his death, I am not sure she knew how to navigate life, but I was there with her. We were both heartsick. My grandmother asked me to lose weight, because she was worried that I would die also. She said that being fat could give me a heart attack too.

When my grandmother became ill toward the end of her life, I sat on her bed in the nursing home. To my knowledge, she was never diagnosed, but I am sure she had Alzheimer's. I taped many of our last conversations, which was our little secret. I listened to them for years after she died. One day, she told me that her mother and sister had visited her the night before and had sat on the edge of her bed. I believed her. She died the next day. My hero, who protected me and loved me, was gone. To this day, I still think about her and my grandfather.

My mother must have known that her in-laws had stepped in to love and nurture me, to be to me what she could never be. This was probably another point of denial and guilt. Again, if she admitted what she was doing, she would have to face her moral failure toward me, my brother, herself — and God. I think that's why she left the church without complaint. She felt her punishment was justified.

Our families form our understanding of ourselves, the world, and what we can expect in life — for good or bad — depending on what we do about it. Eventually, I had to do something about what I thought and how I would respond to everything that had happened to me, had not happened to me, or had been said or implied to me during my childhood and teenage years.

Perhaps the most significant of all was the haunting memory of my mother's shadow, streaming under the bed-room door, as she carried a basket of clothes down the hall — while Marsh assaulted me. She had to have known what was happening. When she attended therapy sessions with me, I knew by the way she reacted to the therapist's questions that her denial was deeper than I imagined. The therapist told me it was too much for her to handle.

As an adult who has worked through so many issues of fear, rejection, and abandonment, I have a much better under-standing of why my mother acted the way she did. Although there are moments when I still feel the hurt and anger toward her, the memories no longer haunt or debilitate me.

When I have these moments, I know I have a choice. That alone is freedom! I can pray and receive even deeper healing. I can go out for a run, call a friend, or even see a trusted therapist if I need to. These are my coping mecha-nisms today. I no longer want to binge to *numb and deny* my pain; I do what is good for me to *rid myself* of the pain. And the best part is, I get to share this experience with others and help them rid themselves of their pain and suffering.

My mother was a teen mother. My father wasn't there and didn't give us any support, financially or emotionally. She had few skills. She probably hadn't known a lot of love growing up. In all my prayer, therapy, and thinking through why she passed my bedroom door without intervening, at the end of the day, I have forgiven her. When you carry anger and unforgiveness, the only one it hurts is you. I couldn't have moved on if I hadn't forgiven her.

Most survivors must come to terms with the fact that their mother or father knew and did nothing. The rest must come to terms that, for some reason, their parents had no idea. Either way, our parents need to be forgiven for not protecting us. Some survivors say they accepted blame for the abuse in the hope that their abusing or enabling parent would love them. This is continuing in denial, and if you don't face the truth, you can't forgive and get free of what happened to you. To be fully healed and whole, you must face the truth and forgive.

A mother carries life inside her body and then nurtures and defends that life with every fiber of her being. Many mothers speak of the deep love and devotion they felt before their child was born. Most mothers know, from the moment their child is placed in their arms, that they would gladly die for them if necessary. Unfortunately, this is not everyone's reality. Some mothers are damaged and become steeped in denial. They are nightmares as mothers, but we must forgive them to be healed.

Forgiveness is opening yourself to understand that your mother or father may have done what they did because of their own brokenness or fear. It doesn't mean that what they did was okay, but it allows you to accept that their human frailty played a role in their failing to protect or believe you. Understanding brings compassion, which makes it easier to forgive.

My mother was only sixty-five when she died, and I truly believe I will see her again in Heaven. That is one place where everything is worked out! I believe she and I will have that chance to settle all the issues that hurt us and divided us in this life. In the meantime, forgiveness allows me to let go of the pain in my past.

I forgive you, Mom, for those years of desperately wanting you to love me when you just could not be there for me. I choose to love you and have compassion on you.

Forgiveness is a miracle that brings miraculous results. Because Jesus miraculously chose to forgive me, I can miraculously forgive others and receive miraculous forgiveness as well. In the end, I am free and know that I am loved by Him and by many others.

> *Before you were conceived, I wanted you.*
> *Before you were born I loved you.*
> *Before you were here an hour I would die*
> *for you.*
> *This is the miracle of life.*
> — *Maureen Hawkins*

# 16

# Therapy Circle

My molester was adored and almost acclaimed in my family. They thought he was the father figure to me and my brother, and he rescued my mother and her kids from a life of poverty. He was considered part of our family. When he arrived, money became readily available, and at first, it seemed like I was finally going to feel loved by a father figure and maybe have some structure and security. Obviously, that never happened, but being healed of my past would never have happened if I hadn't decided to speak out and share my story with those who had experienced something similar.

As an adult, I began to form groups of emotional eaters, weight loss groups. After a while, I realized that most of the women in these groups had been victim to some form of abuse. By that time, I had had years of therapy, read relevant books, kept journals, and found my path to wellness. For me, it was simple: keep reminding myself that abuse was not something that only happened to me. I could find the way to help others. I would tell my story to help them, they would tell their stories to help me. We would no longer be captives of silence. We would help each other be free and stay free.

Once I was released from the hospital, I was admitted to an outpatient program at Hannehman Hospital. I was interviewed by the psychologist who ran the group. She handpicked twelve women, who had been raped or sexually molested in some way. It was a closed group, and we were not to talk about anybody's story outside of the group.

We met weekly, and the first week was an eye opener. All the women looked so normal. That first impression dissolved when we each opened our personal Pandora box of horrors. Most of these women had been raped or molested by their fathers while most of their mothers knew. I cringed, wondering what father would do that to their daughter. I felt better knowing that, at least, Marsh was not related to me. Pretty crazy thinking! I thought it was okay because he wasn't my own father. That is how screwed up my thinking was back then.

Only the doctors running the group knew our stories. I heard story after story, week after week, but one woman's story I will never forget. I'll call her Claudia. The rule was that no one was pressured to speak. You could sit and listen or you could speak. Claudia sat directly across from me, so we made eye contact quite a bit; but she sat for weeks and never said a word. In fact, I even forgot her name until she finally spoke.

One session, she began to squirm in her seat and proceeded to tell the most horrific story I had heard. I thought, *This is only in the movies. Writers make this up. This can't be real!* But it was, and I was coming unglued just listening to her. She spoke so quietly and slumped in her chair. Then she began to cry, and we began to cry with her. Her story was our story. She was struggling to get the words out. Her father molested her and her sister and brother. They would all watch, including their mother, while he took turns with them. He continued through the years and threatened each one of them bodily harm if they ever said a word to anyone.

How could we begin to wrap our minds around that? We all shed bitter tears for her and her siblings. I wanted to get up and hold her and tell her it was okay, but it was not okay! She had suffered years of abuse living with parents who were monsters. How could you possibly recover or heal from that unspeakable time? I was not sure.

The group found out the following week that Claudia suffered from multiple personality disorder and had been admitted to an inpatient facility. We never saw her again, but I never forgot her or her story. Since then, I have cried and prayed for her, along with every victim I have known from groups through the years.

Our group continued, and as the weeks went on, I was really beginning to see the light and feel better. This group gave me hope that there was a brighter day on my horizon. More than ever, I knew God was there, and his plans for me were all good.

My mother had agreed to go into therapy with me, and I was thrilled. I believed this would mend our relationship. I was so naïve and, in the end, heartbroken. My therapist brought in another therapist, who was my mother's age, to make her feel comfortable. This was never going to be possible, as she refused to let her guard down and face the truth.

Now, I think back to that day and I feel such compassion for my mother. At the time, however, I was determined to know what she was feeling. It was time to attack the elephant in the room. While I totally understood that my mother was uncomfortable, so was I. It was about to get ugly.

The therapist brought up the abuse issue, and my mother began to feel sick with anxiety. I could feel this from her body language. She squirmed in her chair, and her lips began to quiver. It felt horrible to see her like this, but we had to talk about it if we were going to move forward and repair our relationship. I tried many times to sit with her alone, but she just avoided the issue. All I wanted was for her to acknowledge me and what had happened. Repeatedly, she changed the subject and pretended it never took place.

The therapist asked her how she perceived my childhood, and that is when she said, "My daughter had such a happy childhood."

I responded, "How would you know? You were rarely home and supposed to protect me." With tears in my eyes, I felt my heart break again. I was so hurt by her, but now I know she was hurt more. To her dying day, she never acknowledged my feelings or the truth.

To make me feel better, the therapist told me that my mother was protecting her emotions from a past that was catching up to her inch by inch. This brought me to realize that her life was too painful. She was very aware of what went down time after time and let it happen. She was not going to reconcile with me or admit that she knew what happened, and I was crushed that she would protect the abuser at any cost. In groups I attended, I learned that my mother was no different than many other mothers, who protected the abusers and made the victims believe it was their fault.

At my next therapy session, the therapist said, "When your mother's emotional floodgates open, I would not want to be in the way of that tsunami."

After years of therapy, prayer, and getting help, I can honestly say I am in the best emotional shape of my life. The reason is because I forgave my mother and my abuser by feeling real compassion toward them. I never would have developed that compassion without the valuable time spent in therapy circles. Hearing other women's stories was the only way I could realize the inadequacies of my mother and abuser and put them in a healthy perspective.

I also had to forgive others, who had hurt me when I was overweight. People would drive by as I was walking down the street and call me names. I remember my great aunt telling me I was fat. Overweight kids are tormented for just looking different, and I can really empathize with their pain and humiliation. I would always laugh off the rude comments to cover my intense hurt and shame.

In various groups of women like me, I was able to understand more clearly what had happened to me. I wasn't unique, it wasn't my fault, and my abuser and enabler (my mother) were not normal. They were the sick ones who made me sick, but I could make choices to get well. God wanted me well, and he would help me. My therapist and the other women wanted me well, and they would help me. I was no longer alone, and the path to recovery grew brighter and brighter.

Today, I thank God for these groups and have started many myself. I know the value of sharing our lives. It is how we become whole, take our place in the world, and make it a better place for being there.

# 17

# I Asked God to Help Me Forgive

*B*eing raised in the Catholic Church, I was taught to confess my sins in private to the priest, receive forgiveness, and do the penance he assigned. The emphasis was on my sin, my guilt, my shame, and my responsibility to get to Heaven by doing right instead of wrong; and if I did wrong, to confess and do the penance. My salvation depended on me. When I gave my life to Jesus Christ at Happy Church, my salvation was on Jesus. He died a terrible death to pay for my sins and made it possible for God to forgive me, for me to forgive myself, and for me to forgive others. I am saved and forgiven not because I live a perfect life but because Jesus lived a perfect life and died in my place, paying my debt for my sin. He satisfied God's justice for me, for all of us.

As a child locked in shame, it never crossed my mind to forgive myself. Today, as an adult, I am quick to forgive myself! If Jesus could forgive *me*, then I can forgive me. If he forgives *me*, then I can forgive others. Forgiveness is central to the Christian faith, but it is also found in other religions and philosophies of life. That is because the results are often miraculous in the way forgiving someone can change your life.

Forgiveness is characteristically defined as the process of letting go of anger or resentment that resulted from a perceived offense, and it involves no longer demanding punishment or restitution from the offender. Anger and resentment are emotions that sap our energy and prevent us from being able to move forward toward our goals and dreams. When we let go of those negative emotions, we free our minds and spirits to create something wonderful. The energy we invested in hatred is now available to help us heal.

There are many different religious views on the topic of forgiveness. Christianity focuses on the need to forgive, so believers may receive divine mercy and be healed of the pain of the offense. Judaism teaches that the person who wronged you must sincerely apologize and take what action they can to right the wrong before they can be forgiven. In Buddhism, forgiveness is a practice that prevents harmful thoughts from damaging your mental well-being or karma.

Research indicates that people who forgive tend to be healthier and happier than those who do not. They have stronger cardiovascular and nervous systems. Studies at Stanford University found that those who were taught to forgive — including people from Northern Ireland, whose loved ones were killed during the political violence there — became less angry and hurt and more positive, compassionate, and self-confident. They also reported having more energy and less stress in their lives.

As significant as it is to forgive others who wronged us, it is just as important to forgive ourselves. Women can have great difficulty doing this. We may let others off the hook, but we continue to punish ourselves. It seems easier to shove those memories down and drown them out with food or some other substance. While we may be understanding and compassionate toward others, we are ruthless and cruel to ourselves when we take any misstep.

By not forgiving yourself, you are holding on to a flawed way of control. Thinking that you brought about the abuse through your weakness or stupidity, you need only to improve your own judgment or behavior to protect yourself in the future. The problem with applying this thinking to your victimization is that you fail to understand the predator.

Abusers are often quite clever in their selection of victims: the kid with a single mom, the latchkey child, the nerdy kid, the needy kid, the kid least likely to tell or be believed if they do tell. There is a grooming process as the predator gains the victim's confidence and ensures their silence. They carefully manipulate the child by making them believe the sexual abuse was partly their idea. After all, sex can feel good, and predators use this as proof to the child that they are complicit.

Predators know those kids who can easily be made to believe that they are to blame. The abuser may also offer their victim the kind of individual attention or material gifts that may be scarce in the child's life. The scenario would be confusing to anyone. But make no mistake, this confusion was carefully planned by the abuser, who also instills fear of the consequences should their victim tell anybody.

In adult cases where sexual trauma is the result of domestic abuse, women blame themselves with questions of, "Why did I choose this man? Why didn't I see who he really was? Why didn't I leave the first time he hurt me? After all, I am an adult not a child, and I should know better." But men who batter women also carefully choose and manipulate their partners.

First, abusive men are often able to recognize a woman who grew up with few healthy boundaries or experienced abuse in her family. Then there is frequently the "sweep you off your feet courtship," with flowers and candlelight. Before your feet touch the ground, there is usually pressure to make the connection more serious. "Move in with me," or "Marry me." There may be a quick trip to the altar before you have time to figure out who this guy really is.

Whether the trauma was the result of adult domestic abuse, childhood abuse, or some sexual assault, victims do tend to blame themselves. The beginning of my inner healing was when Glen said to me, "Let's be clear about this. *You* didn't have sex with anyone. *You* were a child who was violated by an adult." When I embraced the truth that it was not my fault, I began to forgive myself and love myself.

Forgive yourself for everything. Forgive yourself with the same love and compassion that you would offer a dear friend. Forgive yourself for:

- believing you invited the abuse;
- thinking your action or inaction caused what happened to you;
- not telling your parents, pastor, friend, the police, or your loved ones;
- believing you could have stopped it sooner, so you must have liked it;
- thinking that the abuse was a sign that there was something wrong with you;
- responding to the trauma by abusing yourself with food; and

- blaming yourself for what you have lost through abuse, your addiction, or obesity.

For all these reasons, after Jesus forgave me for all my sins and bad decisions, I decided to begin the process of forgiving myself. "I'm sorry for the way I treated myself for so many years. I'm sorry for allowing myself to be covered in fat and making myself feel so unimportant. I'm sorry for letting my weight get in the way of many friendships. I am sorry for hurting myself for years by eating until I could not breathe, sometimes to the point of getting physically sick. I am sorry for binging to cover up all the pain in my life. I am sorry for denying my problems and refusing to face my fears and pain.

"I am sorry for allowing myself to wake up every day, feeling so horribly bad about myself. I forgive myself for buying into the negative way people talked to me and treated me, for creating a toxic environment that allowed me to pity myself instead of changing what was in my power to change. I am sorry for not listening to the wisdom of myself and others and for the hate that I poured into myself as a young girl. I'm sorry for not understanding and forgiving the mother who did not protect me and the man who stole my innocence. I am sorry for letting other people hurt me, and I am sorry for blaming myself and hating myself for the times I was too young to stop people from hurting me."

Once I forgave myself, it was a little easier to forgive others. Forgiving myself required me to understand why I did the things I did, and it gave me more understanding and compassion for myself and for those who had hurt me. The most important and perhaps the hardest was forgiving the one person who was supposed to protect me and chose not to. One of the most difficult things to come to terms with is that your mother or father or older sibling knew, or suspected the abuse, but did nothing. But I was determined to be free. "I forgive you, Mom, for those years of desperately wanting you to love me when you just could not." I chose, again and again until the pain was gone, to stop blaming my mother and believe she had done the best she could.

I gave my anger to God. I prayed, "Please Lord, take my anger away and help me move forward with my life. I pray for you to bring peace to my heart and help me move on. Thank you, Jesus. I love you with all my heart and appreciate my life." Every day, I try to re-commit myself to him and do the best I can to make my life more meaningful. I thank him for helping me to continue moving forward on my path in life. Whenever someone hurts or offends me, I pray; and he helps me forgive.

Those of us who were abused as children or traumatized as adults are certainly entitled to feel bitter. The wrongs committed against us, especially by family members, certainly appear to be the kinds of transgressions that could rightly never be forgiven. But there is a terrible consequence to refusing to forgive: anger and bitterness consume your life and rob you of so much joy and happiness. Anger and bitterness are heavy burdens to carry, especially for a child. Women seeking to heal from abuse and addiction can find themselves buried in a resentment they can't escape.

In an ideal world, our abusers would be found out and face justice. They would admit the wrong they had done, express regret, and make restitution. But few cases end with that kind of resolution. More often, we are left alone with no satisfaction. We must go forward and heal with or without the abuser ever acknowledging their offense. Whatever the circumstances, we much choose to forgive if we are going to break free of our painful past.

There is a misconception that forgiveness may be interpreted as a sign of weakness or surrender, but it is a tool that reveals great courage and strength. By forgiving those who have committed a wrong against us, we come face-to-face with evil and block it from having control over us, thus gaining peace and well-being. In this way, forgiveness creates transformation. God is good, and he loves to bless us when we choose to be good to one another, but especially when we forgive and are good to those who have wronged us.

Jesus tells us to love one another. As a Christian, I truly believe that is how to approach life. He said to love your neighbor as yourself, so that means loving yourself too. Once you love yourself, you can more easily love and forgive others. When the Holy Spirit told me, "You have to forgive Marsh in order to move forward and feel free," I knew he would heal me if I just prayed. If I held that bitterness inside, I was only hurting myself. I had to forgive the man who violated me, but it took a long time and a lot of prayer for this to happen. This was between the Lord and me, and he guided me through it until I was free.

There are so many hurting women, who don't have any idea how to forgive themselves or others. They have no spiritual support from a community or family, where they can tell their story and move through the process of forgiving. If you are one of them, please join a group or find a spiritual leader, where you can share your story, forgive, and be healed.

I firmly believe that one day, you will share your story of healing with others and help them to forgive. Knowing you are not alone in this can be cathartic. When we hear each other's stories, something powerful happens: We are bound together with a deep love and compassion and enter into the miracle of forgiveness, discovering the amazing person God created us to be.

# 18

# "I Will Stand Tall and Proud"

For some of us, being silenced seemed like a punishment equal to the molestation. I was so distraught over my past, for a while I was obsessed with getting even. I sought legal counsel to punish my mother and Marsh, but the statute of limitations had run out, and once again I felt defeated. The lawyer said the same thing my first therapist had said to me: It was not my fault, and at least I could still have my dignity after what they did to me.

It was a gorgeous summer day when I left the lawyer's office, tears streaming down my face. The inner critic began to whisper, and feelings of shame surfaced. I felt so broken. I began to pray and ask God to help me find the serenity I desperately needed. Over time, I began to feel peaceful and less vengeful. Eventually, after much forgiving, I felt sorry for them both. They were trapped in their dysfunction, and that was punishment enough.

At this writing, in my sixties, I still can ask, "Will I ever *totally* heal?" With nothing to hide now, writing and speaking the truth has begun that process. I feel the dignity I always needed. I know the truth and have written about what happened to me. Sometimes I relive those horrific events from years ago, but they no longer have power over me. I want to be loud and clear: You are not defined by your past!

My voice has been central to my well-being as a woman and crucial to my overall health. I pray I energize you to speak out too. I will continue to tell my story to whomever wants to hear it. I encourage you to find your voice, tell your story, and then you will find peace and lead others to peace.

I have survived sexual abuse, binge eating, bulimia, morbid obesity, co-dependent relationships, physical and mental abuse, homelessness, depression, self-hatred and suicidal thoughts. I reclaimed my sanity and began the journey of really living my life. Today, after years of soul searching, journaling, crying, forgiving myself and others, sadness, and anxiety, I emerge as a diamond in the rough. There have been many times that I wanted to give up. It has been a fierce struggle not to revert to my old self-defeating habits, but through determination, self-motivation, and the grace of God, I stay fit and healthy.

My mind has been a great weapon in my battle with food. I taught myself mental skills of meditation, self-talk, and positive imagery. I learned to start with a small goal, visualize it happening, and do whatever it takes to make it happen. This mental process works for me today. I imagine myself overcoming any obstacle in my path. I have conversations with myself: "Can you stick with exercise? I can and I must. Moving and breathing is essential to rebuilding my self-esteem, physical health, and securing my recovery."

I got real with myself and my relationship with food, crushed the inner critic, and began to make wiser decisions. I studied nutrition and adopted a healthy style of eating, which enabled me to let go of my food addiction. I learned the joy of moving my body, no matter what shape and weight it was. When I began to feel better, the struggle within me eased.

I earned a master's degree and lost over 150 pounds. Even now, as an athletic size 12, I do not fit the Hollywood ideal of a pre-pubescent, "single digit" body type; but I am strong, healthy, and I like the way I look. I will never be skinny, but I am totally comfortable with my body.

I have learned to love me just as I am, with all my imperfections.

I have learned to feel my emotions and not eat because of them, which is probably my biggest accomplishment to date.

I have learned to let go of negative feelings and thoughts and move forward.

I have learned to deal with my problems, especially the ones I cannot control.

I have learned to stand up for myself, which was vital to stop eating compulsively.

I have learned that what people do or say has no power over me but my choices that determine my journey in life.

I have learned to give up trying to control others.

I have learned the value of a relationship with God.

I have learned the miracle results of loving and forgiving myself and others.

My journey to health and well-being has given me emotional relief and personal freedom. It has allowed me to be positive about each new day. I have a set of skills that bring me success, and I am sharing them with women everywhere. My passion is to see them conquer yo-yo dieting and obsessing about food. Like me, they will see that food is the fuel we need to drive our lives in high gear. Food is no longer the enemy.

Today, I eat to live instead of living to eat. I make the effort to stay committed to my health. I have changed my life and pour everything I know into others, to motivate them to recover if they choose to.

I do live in the real world and have experienced a few bumps in the road. Relapse is always a possibility, but now I get why I relapse, can forgive myself, and avoid all the shame and blame of the past. I pray and return to positive self-talk until I get my eating under control again. I don't beat myself up for temporarily losing focus, because I have healthy tools to get back to good habits as quickly as possible. Most importantly, I have people to turn to for support and encouragement.

I accept myself as lovable, passionate, with a desire to keep learning while I am alive, and love this excerpt from my journal, dated September 16, 1991: "I will stand tall and proud and know what was done to me." I had been out of the psychiatric hospital for five days and had to make the decision to live consciously. That was and still is the only reasonable choice for me.

Today, I see the journey and am no longer quite so concerned with the destination. I am blessed with friends and family, whom I love dearly, and they are there when it counts. I am closer to God than ever before, and that has really filled a void in me. I am truly living my life's purpose, desiring all women to enjoy the good health and freedom they deserve. I fill my life with the things that matter most.

What matters most to you? Fill your world with those things! Louisa May Alcott wrote, "Far away there in the sunshine are my highest aspirations. I may not reach them, but I can look up and see their beauty, believe in them, and try to follow them."

Is it time to change your future? You do not need another diet! It is time to trust yourself. Feeling fear, anger, frustration, or resentment is to be expected when trying something new. Open yourself to taking the suggestions of people who have been where you are now. Try a different approach. Find a mentor, therapist, or professional who can support you. Join groups that can help you find who you really are and love you along the way. Keep a food journal. Be accountable. It may feel very strange to think about sharing your struggles, but you need to do it. This is your life!

Change will happen when you are ready for it. When your suffering becomes great, it is a sign that you are probably there. But then what? Get the help you need. Recovering from any addiction is a process, and very few people are successful at handling it by themselves. My story will help you see what change can look like, but take your time and find your own, unique path to healing. Changing too quickly can create anxiety and lead you to binge. Take small steps and track them in your journal. It will be easier to make change permanent if you really take your time — and celebrate every step you take.

Make a good plan. You must set realistic, attainable goals for yourself, short-term and long-term, and figure out how you are going to achieve them. Include affirmations. "I am an active woman. I move and breathe three days a week, and I am getting stronger as I do so. I trust myself. I help others and give back to those who help me. I meditate daily and am in touch with my deepest self. I am honest, and fear will have no power over me. My mind creates my reality." Keep your written goals and affirmations where you can see them every day. Stay on track, and when you achieve small victories, make sure you congratulate yourself.

Making changes will take us out of a dysfunctional comfort zone to create a healthy comfort zone, which consists of habits that are healing. Still, for a while you may feel uncomfortable or sad. There will probably be some anxiety too. You are saying goodbye to the food and behaviors that have comforted you for so long. I felt like I was losing my best friend, and so might you.

It helps to envision an active lifestyle, where you are free from compulsive eating and fad diets forever. Visualize a life where you care for yourself and possess the energy you need to live a healthy, happy, and fulfilled life. Picture yourself accepting your body, even if you do not believe it right away. Find the fun in your life. Don't get stuck in a routine where your only movement is trudging on a treadmill. Find activities that are fun and give you a workout.

Take a dance class, climb, ride a bike, hit tennis balls, or put on bathing suit and go swimming. Play has been shown to improve your body, mind, and soul. If you haven't been comfortable in your body, playing can be very freeing. Time to reinvent yourself. You will let your spirit flow, open your mind, and increase your energy. If your childhood was cut short by sad events, then encourage yourself to play in a way that you were not able to as a kid.

I love when I am complimented on how I look. Wanting to feel attractive and liking what you see when you look in the mirror is a normal human desire. The way you present yourself to the world says something about how you feel about yourself. Get up daily, shower, and get dressed like you are going out. Do not sit in baggy, old sweat clothes all day. Even if you not going anywhere, act like you are. Take pride in who you are. Invest in your appearance, because looking nice affects your self-image and mood. This will help you accept and love yourself just as God loves you: unconditionally.

Trauma doesn't have to define you. It doesn't have to rule your life. You don't have to live your life in shame and fear. It's okay to acknowledge who you are. It's okay to acknowledge the past and to move on. Realize that food is not real comfort. Find the strength within you to let things go. You can't control your past, but you can deal with your past and heal from it so that your future is bright with possibility. The challenge is to not define yourself by your weight. You are not a size 18 or a size 20. You are a person with infinite potential for love, joy, and a successful and fulfilled life.

I have lived my life with great gusto and have no regrets. The past has molded me into who I am today. I feel great about myself, my self-esteem and self-worth are at a peak, and I feel great most of the time. I can walk down the street with confidence. I'm no longer that scared, fat, lonely girl who had nowhere to find peace from the sins of her past. The trauma of the abuse has wedged itself in a vague corner deep in my soul. Once I came to terms with the confusion, sadness, and shame, I had to believe that I could live free of the trauma that caused them.

What happened to me as a child was tragic, and I have spent a lot of time asking God why it happened. Today, I have an answer. I see the bigger picture now. He has used me and all my experiences to heal and restore many, many others like me. There's nothing more fulfilling than that! And each year, as the events of my childhood fade more and more, my life carries much more significance. No longer *Eating My Secrets*, I face life with happiness and anticipation, thrilled to see the sunrise each day. This is my prayer for you too!

*Light tomorrow with today.*
   *– Elizabeth Barrett Browning*